LADY

OTHER STORIES OF FAMOUS TEXANS
BY THE AUTHOR

WILLIAM BARRET TRAVIS: *Victory or Death*

JIM BOWIE: *A Texas Legend*

STEPHEN F. AUSTIN: *The Father of Texas*

JAMES BUTLER BONHAM: *The Rebel Hero*

JAMES W. FANNIN: *Remember Goliad*

LADY

A Biography Of

Claudia Alta (Lady Bird) Johnson, Texas' First Lady

By

Jean Flynn

EAKIN PRESS ★ Austin, Texas

FIRST EDITION

Published in the United States of America
By Eakin Press
An Imprint of Sunbelt Media, Inc.
P.O. Drawer 90159   ★   Austin, TX 78709-0159

ISBN 0-89015-821-5

Library of Congress Cataloging-in-Publication Data

Flynn, Jean.
    Lady : the story of Claudia Alta (Lady Bird) Johnson, Texas' First Lady /
by Jean Flynn.
        p.   cm.
    Summary: Discusses the early years, marriage, and political campaigns
and projects of Lady Bird Johnson.
    ISBN 0-89015-821-5 : $14.95
    1. Johnson, Lady Bird, 1912 – — Juvenile literature. 2. Johnson, Lyn-
don B. (Lyndon Baines), 1908–1973 — Juvenile literature. 3. Presidents —
United States — Wives — Biography — Juvenile literature. [1. Johnson,
Lady Bird, 1912– . 2. First ladies.] I. Title.
E848.J64F58   1991
973.923′092 — dc20
[B]   91-19321
                                                                                  CIP
                                                                                   AC

For my sisters,
Pat Byrd and Catherine Hill

Contents

Foreword

Jean Flynn saw a need and met it. The librarian at Sam Rayburn Middle School in San Antonio has long been an admirer of Lady Bird Johnson, but she found no biography of this remarkable and beloved First Lady which was aimed at the thousands of seventh- to tenth-graders. Ms. Flynn's book, *Lady,* is the result of months of research into everything written about the Texas-born First Lady. It is, as far as I know, the only juvenile biography of Mrs. Johnson. She has been included in collections but never singled out.

This is not Jean Flynn's first book. Texas heroes have had the benefit of her research and writing, with similar biographies of Travis, Bowie, Austin, Fannin, and Bonham.

Lady Bird is her first heroine, and she begins with her birth and naming in Karnack, Texas, on December 22, 1912, through school and the University of Texas and on to become the wife of Lyndon Johnson, her widowhood, and the launching of a beautification movement and the National Wildflower Research Center.

To guide students who are unfamiliar with Lady Bird's trails through politics, the issues of the Great Society, through countless visits to Appalachia, the author includes a glossary of definitions such as "aesthetic, bobbed hair, Ku Klux Klan, filibusterer," and the alphabet agencies of the New Deal, "NYA and WPA."

What will intrigue today's young adults will be the

fact that the impressive and lovely First Lady we see today emerged from a lonely motherless childhood in rural East Texas and was never one of the stylish "clique," during her school days. She used her alone time to observe and delight in the beauty around her, to let it enhance her life, and as she entered the world of power, to bring her love of beauty to the nation's conscience and improve our treatment of the world we live in. She makes an inspiring lasting mark on her family and country by a life well lived.

A great many teenagers are going to feel a new sense of esteem and purpose with this story.

LIZ CARPENTER

Preface

Lindy Boggs, wife of Congressman Hale Boggs, said ". . . this is the problem with Bird. When you talk about her, you make her too good to be true." The Johnsons' long-time friend and Speaker of the House Sam Rayburn said, "Lady Bird is unmatchable, too good to be true."

The difficulty in writing this book came in trying to present Lady Bird Johnson as a person with human frailties as well as her good qualities. I decided to let her speak for herself and to let others who know her speak about her. The book is a combination of facts and direct quotes taken from printed interviews and oral histories. Footnotes or notes become burdensome to many readers; therefore, I have omitted them. Many of the quotes are repeated in several works listed in the bibliography.

Lady Bird Johnson expressed a wish that a biography not be written until after her death. This book was not written with lack of respect for her wishes, but so that future generations of young people may understand her influence on the environmental movement in America. It is my wish that this book may bridge that gap.

CHAPTER 1

Birth of a Lady

"Why, she's as purty as a lady bird," said the black nursemaid Alice Tittle as she gently rocked the baby. Alice was comparing the beauty of the baby's dark eyes to those of the ladybird beetles of the East Texas region.

The actual time that Claudia Alta Taylor took on her nickname, Lady Bird, is not clear. Some reports have said the incident happened the day she was born and others report it was when she was two. The nickname stayed with her even though she tried to change it. When no one would call her Claudia, she tried spelling her name Byrd, but it was all in vain. She remained "Lady Bird."

Claudia Alta Taylor was born on December 22, 1912, in Brick House in Karnack, Texas. The small town in Harrison County, near the Louisiana border, had only about 100 residents at the time. Lady Bird was the only one of the three Taylor children to be born in Brick House. She was named after her mother's brother, Claude Patillo, a relatively wealthy bachelor who lived in Alabama and eventually made Lady Bird his sole heir.

Lady Bird was the third child born to Thomas Jeffer-

Claudia Taylor with her nursemaid, Alice Tittle.
— Courtesy LBJ Library

son and Minnie Lee Taylor. Thomas J. (Tommy) III was
eleven and Antonio (Tony) was eight years old when she
was born. They were always begging to spend the night
with the Haley brothers, who lived about two miles from
them, and were not allowed to go often. The night before
Lady Bird was born, they were sent to stay the night with
their friends. Tony Taylor said, "We knew something was
about to happen, but we didn't know what. We hadn't
even asked to spend the night but we were willing to go
without a fuss!"

Lady Bird's ancestry can be traced back to Spanish-
Scottish on her mother's side and English on her father's
side. Her parents had very different personalities. They
had married despite the objections of her mother's family, who considered T. J. Taylor to be a "ne're-do-well,
dirt farmer." The young couple had fallen in love when
they were still in school together. The differences in personalities and upbringing, along with Minnie Patillo's
poor health, created tension in the Taylor marriage.

Thomas Jefferson Taylor, the son of an Alabama
sharecropper, moved to Karnack (named after the tem-
ples of Egypt by someone who did not know how to spell)
as soon as he was old enough to support himself. He located across the Texas-Louisiana border in East Texas,
which was reminiscent of the Old South from which he
had come. The area had red clay in its low hills, fetid
swamps, and stagnant, muddy bayous lined with the
gnarled roots of giant, moss-draped cypresses. It was also
similar to the Old South because of the servitude of black
sharecroppers.

He put his robust energies into a flourishing cotton
business and general store, where he proclaimed himself
"T. J. Taylor, Dealer in Everything." He opened a truly
"general" store and then another, and then a cotton gin,
and then another. He later expanded his enterprises by
adding a sawmill and oil and gas leases on his land.

He began accumulating his wealth by loaning
money to sharecroppers, those farmers who owned noth-

ing. Everything was furnished by the owner of the land: the land, seeds to sow, and machinery to work the crop. He offered the sharecroppers credit at the store at an interest as well as loaning them money.

Moneylending at ten percent brought him good returns from those who could pay. He foreclosed on the crops of those who could not pay. With the extra money he made on the sale of the crops, he acquired thousands of acres of land during the first twenty years of the twentieth century.

He built a large, one-story frame house behind the store in Karnack for his bride. The house had several large bedrooms and a library/music room for Minnie Lee. It was in this house that his two sons were born. At the time the house was very impressive because of its size.

Taylor purchased Brick House, in which Lady Bird was born, around 1910. The two-story antebellum structure with columns in front was the most imposing one in or near Karnack. It was constructed of red clay bricks, which had been made by slaves on the plantation before the Civil War.

Thomas Jefferson Taylor was a tall (six-foot-two), stocky, large-handed man who "never talked about anything but making money," and he was tireless in its pursuit. He rose at 4:00 A.M. to open his stores, and after a long day behind the counter, returned home at sundown to spend a long evening toting up accounts and checking the dates on IOUs. During harvest time, he never left his gins until the last wagonload of cotton had been baled. If the baler didn't stop until 1:00 or 2:00 A.M., T. J. still went home to his ledgers.

He was ruthless in his dealings with the sharecroppers. Gene Boehringer Lasseter, who grew up near his home, said, "The Negroes were kept in peonage by Mr. Taylor. He would furnish them with supplies and let them have land to work, then take their land if they didn't pay. When I first saw how he operated, I thought the days of slavery weren't over yet."

Tom Taylor, Lady Bird's brother, said of his father, "He looked on Negroes pretty much as hewers of wood and drawers of water." White men called him "Cap'n Taylor." Blacks called him "Mister Boss."

Taylor bought more and more land. By the time he married Minnie Lee Patillo of Alabama, he owned 18,000 acres, was "Mister Boss" of the whole northern portion of Harrison County, and lived in one of the town's largest houses.

After her native Alabama, East Texas provided a cloistered life for Minnie Taylor. She loved culture and had come to Karnack with trunkloads of beautifully bound books as well as a phonograph and records by Enrico Caruso and various operas. She surrounded herself in an atmosphere of culture, eccentricity, and aloofness from the secluded ways of Karnack. She had her own car and chauffeur. Veils and turbans protected her from the sun and provided relief from migraine headaches. They also gave her a mysterious appearance that the local residents of Karnack were not used to. She went from one food fad to another and avoided meat.

Mrs. Taylor was a misfit in Karnack and escaped the town when she could. She went to Chicago each year for the opera season, and there were other visits to sanitariums in the Midwest for treatment of her nervous disorder. At an early age Tommy and Tony were sent to Alabama to live with different relatives. They spent three years there while Mrs. Taylor was in a sanitarium trying to recover her health. She returned to Alabama, where she and her sons stayed with relatives for another two years, until the boys were old enough to attend school. The three of them then returned to Karnack, where the two boys went to the local public school.

Although there were servants in the Taylor household, eight-year-old Tony babysat with Lady Bird for five cents an hour after she was born. The two boys had to make their own spending money. Tony found babysitting an easy task until Lady Bird became a toddler. Then he had to keep up with her to see she didn't fall down the stairs or wander off into the fields. The boys were pretty much left on their own. Their father was gone long hours, and their mother was absorbed in her activities.

During the early years of the twentieth century, women were not allowed to vote. But Mrs. Taylor still became involved in local interests. She went out in pursuit of black culture in areas where other whites never ventured. She organized a successful drive to protect local quail against excessive hunting. In the last summer of her life (1918), she became involved in local politics. Women still could not vote in the Democratic primary, but Mrs. Taylor campaigned against a candidate who had received a draft deferment. " 'Mr. Bob' " was, she told other women, "a slacker." Women had influence somewhere, because "Mr. Bob" lost the election.

In Karnack, Mrs. Taylor was remembered as "a cultured woman" who "didn't consort with Karnack people." She was loved by her servants and criticized by the neighborhood for her "weird and stand-offish" practice of entertaining blacks. She was interested in black religious practices and once began to write a book which she titled *Bio Baptism*. Her liberal interests were not shared by her husband, although he did not seem to object to her having an open mind.

Mrs. Taylor was not in good health after Lady Bird's birth. Due to her history of nervous disorders, she had been in and out of sanitariums since her marriage. She had a nervous breakdown when Lady Bird was about three years old and recovered in a sanitarium in Battle Creek, Michigan. Tommy and Tony were sent away to boarding schools. Because of the differences in their ages, they were sent to different kinds of schools. Tony remarked in later years about their separation from family: "We were at different schools, far from home. It was easier for Tommy and me to get together on vacation, holidays, or whenever we could than to go home."

After returning home from the sanitarium in Battle

Creek, Mrs. Taylor became pregnant at the age of forty-four. In the late summer of 1918, the family dog tripped her on the stairs. The fall caused a miscarriage, blood poisoning, and death in September of that year.

Lady Bird was quite sure that her mother was going to return. She had gone away before and had always come back, but in time "I [Lady Bird] quit even thinking about it at all. . . I could hear people saying that Mother was gone. I could tell that they were feeling sorry for me, but I thought to myself, 'Well, I know more about that than they do. She'll be back.' "

Lady Bird had only "fleeting impressions" of her mother. She was "tall, graceful, wore white quite a lot, and went around the house in a great rush and loved to read." But she has said, "I remember so many things she read to me. She used to read me Greek, Roman and Teutonic myths. Siegfried, with his magic cloak and sword, was the first romantic hero I ever loved."

Mr. Taylor didn't know what to do with the motherless little girl. Lady Bird was five years old when her mother died. Her brothers were away at school, and aside from black playmates, her mother had been her only companion. For a while, Mr. Taylor took her with him to the store. She played around the store in the daytime and slept on a cot in the attic above the store at night when he worked late. Stacked near the cot where she slept were the coffins that Taylor sold. When she questioned her father about the long wooden "boxes" near her cot, he answered, "Dry goods, honey." She was constantly exposed to the ghost stories of East Texas, and the idea of coffins would have set off her overactive imagination.

The store was Lady Bird's first taste of the world of business, an experience she later put to excellent use. Her father also supplied her with a model of assertive masculinity that later shaped her choice of a husband. "He was head man in his tiny world," she said.

When Lady Bird was six, Mr. Taylor's relatives advised him to send her to Alabama to live with her mother's spinster sister, Effie Patillo. Although Taylor was more than fond of his daughter, he was not willing to leave his business in anyone else's hands to take Lady Bird. He tied a tag around her neck for identification and destination and sent her on a train ride alone to Billingsley, Alabama. She arrived wearing a big French bonnet that framed her dark brown eyes and a soft, shy smile.

She required no one to entertain her or keep her happy, and she soon became the favorite child in the family. Many of the Patillo family were childless and lived within 100 miles of Billingsley. They arranged to transport Lady Bird from one place to another so they all could keep her for short periods of time. According to relatives, she adapted well to the different households. But shyness and quietness were a way of life for her.

Aunt Effie, who soon moved to Karnack, raised Lady Bird. She was a slight, sickly woman. "She opened my spirit to beauty," Lady Bird said about her aunt, "but she neglected to give me any insight into the practical matters a girl should know about, such as how to dress or choose one's friends or learning to dance . . . She was undoubtedly the most otherworldly human in the world. She had a polite musical education considered proper for a young lady of her day, and she played the piano quite well."

Aunt Effie and her mother's beautiful books became Lady Bird's closest companions. The library that Lady Bird inherited from her mother contained books that many Americans regarded as classics in those years. She loved to read and memorized poems that she could recite decades later. Reading by lamplight, she finished *Ben-Hur* at the age of eight. Her Alabama relatives were amazed at the books she could read at such a young age. She read *Tom Sawyer, Huck Finn, Uncle Remus,* and books by Zane Grey and H. Rider Haggard. The H. Rider Haggard books "dipped into the occult and beyond the fringe." She was perfectly happy sitting on the swing on the front porch with a book and munching on dried peaches, dried apricots, or dried figs.

Lady Bird grew up in the comfortable lifestyle of Brick House, whose two stories made it distinctive in Karnack. Brick House did not have running water or electricity for the first few years of Lady Bird's life. She read by lamplight until she was nine. Luxuries would be added with progress, but the house was still the most impressive structure in or around Karnack at that time.

Lady Bird once said of Karnack: "It was a lonesome place, but I wasn't lonely. It's true that I didn't know many youngsters of my own age and background, and that proved difficult later when I had to mingle with others in school. But I had the whole wide world to roam in. And I had Aunt Effie."

She remembered that Effie Patillo was "delicate and airy and very gentle and she gave me many fine values which I wouldn't trade for the world." Among those gifts were a feeling for nature and a devotion to reading, similar to that of Lady Bird's mother. Aunt Effie was less successful on the practical side of life. Lady Bird grew up having to depend on herself in school and on friends of her own age that she made in both Texas and Alabama.

The frail, sickly Effie Patillo had other influences on Lady Bird's life. As she grew older, she felt that some of Aunt Effie's illnesses were psychosomatic. Aunt Effie was often ill when there were no physical reasons. Lady Bird saw how her aunt's life was limited by being so frail and weak. She did not want her own life to be restricted by real or imagined illness. She said, "I set my sights on being more like my father, who was one of the most physically strong people I have ever known."

Much of Lady Bird's time was spent alone out-of-doors. "When I was a little girl, I grew up listening to the wind in the pine trees of the East Texas woods." On Caddo Lake, which was very near Brick House, she "loved to paddle in those dark bayous, where time itself seemed ringed around by silence and ancient cypress trees, rich in festoons of Spanish moss. Now and then an alligator would surface like a gnarled log. It was a place for dreams." On her walks she watched the wildflowers and daffodils in the yard. From her earliest years, she had appreciated the natural landscape. The landscape was not to be conquered or changed. It was to be enjoyed for its own sake.

Lady Bird went to Fern Public School No. 14, a one-room schoolhouse atop a red clay hill near Karnack. She attended school there from the first through the seventh grade and was at one time the only child enrolled. At times she was the only white child in attendance with sharecroppers' children. There were seldom as many as a dozen students, and few of them stayed very long. They were the children of sharecroppers who owed money to Cap'n Taylor and were constantly moving away.

Friday afternoons at school were spent singing patriotic songs the students had learned by heart. The desks were arranged around "a plump stove" in the middle of the room. On wintry mornings the stove was lit by the bigger boys, whose job it was to carry in the logs. Lady Bird loved the school. There were no boarding schools for her as there were for her brothers. She had no desire to leave her father, Aunt Effie, and the surrounding beauty of the countryside.

Lady Bird and Aunt Effie escaped the long, hot Texas summers by visiting relatives in Alabama or making trips as far away as Colorado or Michigan. Reminiscing about her Alabama holidays, Lady Bird said, "I remember the laughing hayrides and watermelon suppers, learning to swim in Mulberry Creek, the lazy curl of a cousin's fishing line flickering in the sun, church on Sunday and then the long Sunday dinner with kinsfolk — endless kinsfolk — discussing the endless family gossip around the table." Her mother's family always welcomed her among them and treated her like the other young people.

Lady Bird was the favorite of Claude Patillo, her

mother's and Aunt Effie's bachelor brother. Mr. Patillo was determined that Lady Bird should one day attend Harvard Business School, which she never did, and insisted that she read books on finance. By the time she was twelve, he had her studying stock-market quotations with the eye of an expert. Although he did not live to witness it, he would have been proud of Lady Bird's keen business insight in later operating her own radio station.

She attended school in nearby Jefferson, Texas, for two years. She and Aunt Effie lived in an apartment in Jefferson and went home on the weekends. During this time she "spelled [her] middle name Byrd, after [she] had given up ever managing to be called Claudia!" She went to Marshall, the county seat, for high school, and graduated at fifteen.

When she first attended Marshall High School, one of her father's employees — a clerk, bookkeeper, and butcher — drove her to school. Her father picked her up in the evenings. Sometimes Mr. Taylor sent her to school in a pick-up filled with cowhides. The cowhides smelled so bad she insisted on getting out at least two blocks from school. She walked the rest of the way and hoped that nobody saw her, or smelled the pick-up.

Her father bought her a Chevrolet coupe after a few weeks because it became too much to arrange transportation for her. She loved it when it rained or snowed and the roads were axle-deep in mud. Then she spent the night in town with Ida Mae Pou or Emma Boehringer. Her friends sometimes spent the night with Lady Bird, and they took picnics from Mr. Taylor's store and went to the pond for "serious studying" in English and math.

But those were not happy, carefree school years for Lady Bird. Years later, when she was reflecting on her high school years, she said, "I don't recommend that to anyone, getting through high school that young. I was still in socks when all the other girls were wearing stockings. And shy — I used to hope that no one would speak to me. There was one boy who used to try to talk to me. He was real nice, and, what's more, he was real glamorous, being on the football team. But I never knew what to say, and finally it got so that if I saw him coming, I'd leave the room.

"I had two heavy crosses to bear in my early teens," she said. "One was my nickname and the other was my hooknose, which at the time I seriously considered having bobbed. I never did and gradually I came to accept both of them."

Although her dark eyes were expressive and her complexion a smooth olive, she was not considered by her classmates to be a pretty girl. Her clothes took away from her attractive qualities. The baggy, drab-colored dresses looked as if they had been handed down from some older and larger woman. Her father would buy her any clothes she wanted, but according to Naomi Bell, a friend who has known Lady Bird since the age of ten, "Bird didn't give a hoot about fancy clothes but always was clean and neat." She was a contrast to the girls with bangs, bobbed hair, short skirts, and several strands of long beads, which was the style in the 1920s.

At school dances, Lady Bird was a wallflower. She had little to talk about with the other girls, who were interested only in the most recent fashions, dancing, and boys. Her classmates remember her as being extremely shy, almost as if she had a fear of meeting or talking to people.

Her friend Naomi Bell said, "Bird wasn't accepted into our clique. [There were eighteen girls in Lady Bird's class.] We couldn't get Claudia to cooperate on anything. She didn't date at all. To get her to go to the graduation banquet, my fiancé took Bird as his date, and I went with another boy. She didn't like to be called Lady Bird, so we'd call her Bird to get her little temper going. When she'd get into a crowd, she'd clam up."

Lady Bird was younger than the crowd that drove around the square on Saturday afternoons to see what everyone else was doing. The square was covered on the west side by wagons and pick-ups and by touring cars on the other sides. Coupe cars with rumble seats were the envy of all the young people. When they had driven around the square enough times to satisfy their curiosity and to let everyone see them, they went to one of the drug stores for a cherry Coke or Delaware Punch to catch up on the gossip.

She did go to movies at "The Grand" with friends. Clara Bow, Will Rogers, Rudolph Valentino, and Tom Mix were favorite movie stars of the young people. When a special event was celebrated, some of the young people drove to Shreveport for an evening at the palatial "Strand Theater." It had to be a special celebration because the tickets cost twenty-five cents per person to attend the shows (at that time a high price).

Lady Bird lost her unhappiness of school in her love of nature. She boated and walked alone. She loved the winding bayous of Caddo Lake, the moss hanging around her as a protective shield from the outside cruelties of the everyday world. She lost herself in "drifts of magnolia all through the woods in the spring and the daffodils in the yard. When the first one bloomed, I'd have a little ceremony, all by myself, and name it the queen."

Her unhappiness in school was not reflected in her grades. She was an excellent student, but even her good grades caused her dread. She was terrorized by the thought that she might finish first or second in her class and have to make a speech at graduation as valedictorian or salutatorian. She prayed that she would finish no higher than third. Then she prayed that if she came in higher than third that she would get smallpox. She would rather risk the scars than stand up before an audience. The final grades were Emma Boehringer, 95; Maurine Cranson, 94½; Claudia Taylor, 94.

Lady Bird was not one of the "clique" of girls, but she was always dependable and frequently was asked to help complete tasks on time. When someone wanted to be sure a task was completed, she was called upon to do it. She took part in school activities and worked on the school newspaper, *The Parrot*. She readily gave hours to build floats for parades, sometimes staying overnight with friends when it was too late for her to drive home alone.

Dorris Powell, who was almost like a mother to Lady Bird in Karnack, and her husband encouraged Lady Bird to bring friends, both boys and girls, to their house on the lake. The Powells chaperoned parties there and did the cooking for the picnics. The young people swam in the lake and played cards and games.

Lady Bird continued her love of reading in high school when it was not a popular thing to do. She read Richard Halliburton's *Royal Road to Romance,* published in 1923. Students teased her about carrying around the book. She wanted to travel even then.

She enjoyed working on the school newspaper and took great pleasure "in seeing my name on a by-line no matter how inconsequential." She did not enjoy the newspaper's joke that her ambition was to "be an old maid." In 1928, when Lady Bird graduated from high school, the class prophet wrote in "Hoo's Hoo in 1928" a prediction that Claudia Alta Taylor would be a "second Halliburton poking her nose in the unknown places in Asia."

It was not until 1961 that she began her extensive world travels and made her first trip into Asia as Mrs. Lyndon B. Johnson, wife of the vice-president of the United States, thus fulfilling the prophecy.

CHAPTER 2

Leaving Karnack

Lady Bird graduated from high school at the age of fifteen without having to go to a boarding school. But that was soon to change. Her father and Aunt Effie decided that she was too young for college and that she should attend St. Mary's Episcopal School for Girls in Dallas. Aunt Effie went with her to Dallas, but because her health was frail, she lived in a nursing home.

St. Mary's was a junior college and an all girls' school. Being in a closed environment did not encourage Lady Bird to develop social skills in dealing with young men. She remarked in later years, "There is a stark loneliness in any boarding school, especially [for] anyone as shy as I."

Lady Bird was not the only shy student at St. Mary's. Most of the girls enrolled in the school were shy because their parents had overprotected them. St. Mary's was an extension to that overprotectiveness. There were other boarding students as well as day students who lived at home.

Emily Crow was a day student from Dallas who be-

Lady Bird's photograph for Lyndon Johnson (about 1934).
— Courtesy LBJ Library

came best friends with Lady Bird. They shared the same love of the outdoors. If they had a choice between being inside or out, they chose outside every time. Lady Bird spent many weekends with the Crow family and became like a family member. Emily had two brothers and one sister who helped ease Lady Bird's shyness.

The girls walked, golfed with Emily's brother, Davis, went horseback riding, and picnicked as often as they could. The Crow household was one of readers, and many books lined their walls. Emily's parents enjoyed lively discussions with the young people about the books they were reading at the time. They offered Lady Bird a family environment that she had not had in Karnack with her father and Aunt Effie.

In turn, Lady Bird offered Emily and her roommate, Helen Bird, a different set of experiences when they went home with her for a visit. Mr. Taylor let them do exciting things that their own fathers would not allow. When they drove down the dirt roads from Brick House, he allowed the girls to stand on the running board of the car or ride on the fenders. They were never allowed to do that in the city. They were turned loose on horses to ride anywhere they wanted. And Lady Bird took them to her father's store, where he told them to choose whatever they wanted for their picnics on Caddo Lake.

The store which "dealt in everything" was a new experience for the city girls. They loved the smells of fertilizer, tobacco, mints, candy, cheese, and new cut cloth that permeated the store. They liked the old men who sat around a table and played dominoes and teased them. They envied Lady Bird's freedom "to choose whatever you want for your picnic." But they admired her for choosing only those things that would be eaten: crackers, cheese, drinks, and cookies. Even then she was not wasteful.

When they really felt daring, they went skinny-dipping in Caddo Lake. Emily and Helen were frightened by the alligators in the water, but that did not keep them from swimming. They visited with Dorris Powell and read aloud to each other from current magazines. Whether the girls were in Dallas or in Karnack, they enjoyed all of the outdoor activities they could manage in a weekend.

In the two years at St. Mary's, Lady Bird intensified her love of the theater by seeing plays at the Dallas Little Theater and by taking roles in school productions. One of the characters she played was Sir Toby Belch in *Twelfth Night*. Another part was the butler in *The Importance of Being Earnest*. Her interest in drama helped ease her shyness while she was in Dallas. On stage she lost herself in the role of another character.

She continued to read voraciously and complained with the other students about the restrictions that a girls' school imposed on its students. The girls at St. Mary's had a song that expressed their views of their lives at the school:

> "Root-a-toot-toot, root-a-toot-toot.
> We're the girls from the institute.
> We don't smoke and we don't chew,
> And we don't go with boys who do.
> Our class won the Bible!"

As Effie Patillo became more frail, she wanted Lady Bird to go to Alabama with her and finish school there. Lady Bird's friend, Eugenia (Gene) Boehringer, pleaded against it. She invited Lady Bird to visit her in Austin and to look at the University of Texas before she made a decision. There was never any question about Lady Bird's desire to go to college. The only conflict was where she was to go, and she wanted to finish school in her own state.

She flew from Dallas to Austin in 1930, although she hated flying, to look over the University of Texas. "I fell in love with Austin the first moment that I laid eyes on it and that love has never slackened," she said in later years. Part of its appeal was its natural beauty. The city of Austin, the capital of Texas, is located on both sides of a bend in the Colorado River in central Travis County. Its rolling hills give it a sense of smallness of community but an openness to nature. "There were bluebonnets with red poppies and primroses among them. I remember them like a friend!" That trip determined Lady Bird's decision to attend the University of Texas.

T. J. Taylor had continued to accumulate wealth despite the onset of the Great Depression. He furnished Lady Bird with her own car, a black Buick which "wasn't old but was not new," and an unlimited charge account at Neiman-Marcus. But for whatever reason, he refused to allow her to join Alpha Phi sorority, which she pledged as a freshman. Her fellow pledges could tell that she was very disappointed, but she never explained why her father refused or criticized him for it. It was unlike him to refuse Lady Bird anything.

Lady Bird lived near the campus in one of the best roominghouses in the area. Her roommate was Cecille Harrison. They shared a double bed in one of the three bedrooms Mrs. Matthews rented in her home. It was considered a roominghouse instead of a boardinghouse because Mrs. Matthews fixed only breakfast as a part of their monthly fee. Lady Bird and Cecille ate most of their other meals at Wukasch's, a half-block away from the house. They purchased lunch tickets but occasionally took their dinner meal at another restaurant. It was obvious to the other students that Lady Bird had money, but she did not call attention to it. She was well-liked by those who knew her.

She had studied history at St. Mary's with Frances Miller, who instilled in her a respect and affection for the subject that put her "on a lifetime program as a history student." Along with her history major at the university, she added a concentration in journalism. She also took a course in geology "which stretched my perspective of life of man on this physical planet." She studied to be a teacher, which seemed a respectable profession for a

Southern girl who might become an old maid like her
Aunt Effie Patillo.

At the university, she was still shy, almost as with-
drawn as she had been in high school. Despite the unlimited charge account her father had opened for her at Neiman-Marcus, she still dressed in flat-heeled, sensible,
plain shoes and big, plain dresses. Her only coat was an
old coat of her Aunt Effie's. While her clothes still reflected her preference for drab colors and flat, comfortable shoes, pictures of her at this time reflect a slender,
stylish young woman.

Her shyness sometimes seemed to be a losing battle.
Since Gene Boehringer had encouraged Lady Bird to
come to Austin, she felt somewhat responsible for her.
Gene had known Lady Bird for several years, although
she was the older of the two. Emma, Gene's sister, graduated from Marshall High School the same year as Lady
Bird. Emma and Gene's mother, a widow with six children, taught the children they did not need money to be
wealthy. Lady Bird had been younger and wealthier than
the sisters in high school, but she was sometimes included in the Boehringers' activities.

The Boehringer children were all encouraged to go to
school, even though they had to work their way through
a little at a time. Gene had been in Austin since 1926.
She had attended two years at College of Marshall and
earned a teacher's certificate, but she did not want to
stay in Marshall. When the opportunity to work in Austin presented itself, she accepted the job. She was secretary to Railroad Commissioner C. V. Terrell and attended classes around her work schedule. Mr. Terrell
realized what a good worker she was and allowed her to
come to work late for a morning class or come to work
early and take a class during a long lunch period. She
also enrolled in evening classes. Although she was a hard
worker, Gene loved a good time and encouraged Lady
Bird to become less reserved.

"Gene made me feel important for the first time,"

Lady Bird said. "She was one of those tremendously out-going people who made everyone around her feel a little more alive. I am a friendlier, more confident person today because of Gene."

Gene herself did not see much, if any, confidence in her friend. After trying in vain to get her to buy more colorful clothes, Gene called Lady Bird, in exasperation, "stingy." Although Gene was exasperated at Lady Bird's appearance, she observed that "She [Lady Bird] always had a lot of young men, you know, beaus in those days."

Two of her boyfriends observed glimpses of a strong character beneath the quietness of the young woman. "For a while," said Thomas C. Soloman, "I thought I was the leader." But he came to realize that that impression was incorrect. "We had been doing what she wanted to do. Even when we went on a picnic, it was she who thought up the idea. This convinced me that it would take a strong man to be the boss. I also knew she would not marry a man who did not have the potentiality of becoming somebody."

J. H. Benefield came to realize that the shy, reserved young woman "was one of the most determined persons I met in my life, one of the most ambitious and able. She confided in me her wish to excel."

"Claudia made it clear," Emily Crow said, "that she was really never serious about anybody who she thought wouldn't amount to something, wouldn't work hard and get there."

Lady Bird continued to pursue activities that kept her outside as often as possible. Emily Crow, who was one year behind her, moved to Austin in 1931. Their activities became an extension of those at St. Mary's, except now they included boys. Along with Cecille and young men and women, they went on picnics at Bull Creek and Hamilton's Pool and went horseback riding, which was one of Lady Bird's favorite outdoor sports. They boated and swam in the Colorado River. Occasionally a group of men and women drove to San Antonio's

Majestic Theater to see a show. They made trips to Nuevo Laredo for a weekend away from studies. As Gene stated, "There were many beaux, but no one special person" in Lady Bird's life during those university days. She still spent more time with her girlfriends than with boyfriends.

Lady Bird showed the same ambition and determination at the university as she did at Marshall High School. She graduated in 1933 with a bachelor of arts degree with honors and a second-grade teacher's certificate.

Her father and aunt expected her to return to Karnack, but she did not want to go home to live. Her summers during college had been spent in Karnack and Alabama with one trip to Colorado. One summer had been spent at Tuscaloosa at the University of Alabama. She had passed most of the time in leisure: reading, walking, and visiting with friends and relatives. But at the university she had discovered "all the doors of the world suddenly were swung open to me." She did not want to return to the small, secluded world of Karnack.

Another door that had been opened to her during her years in Austin was the Episcopal church. She had attended the church at St. Mary's Episcopal School in Dallas, but she pursued her interest in the Episcopalian faith while she was in Austin. She was raised a Methodist and her father contributed a considerable amount of money to that church. He also contributed to the Baptist church in Karnack. Lady Bird was confirmed at St. David's Episcopal Church in 1933, where she had attended during her student days.

In the summer of 1933, after her graduation, she and Gene Boehringer went to Taos, New Mexico. From Taos they went to Santa Fe to visit Lady Bird's brother Tony and his wife Elizabeth. Elizabeth had graduated from Marshall High School the same year as Gene and they were friends. That gave Lady Bird an excuse to get to know her brother because they had not spent much time together when they were growing up. The trip began a closer bond between the brother and sister.

Lady Bird returned to the university for an extra year and received a second degree in journalism "because I thought that people in the press went more places and met more interesting people, and had more exciting things happen to them."

She fought her shyness because a journalist could not be shy. She became a reporter for the *Daily Texan* and forced herself to ask questions at press conferences. She volunteered to be public relations manager of the university's intramural sports association which oversaw women's athletics. A journalism assignment that she wrote on the poems of John Keats appeared in the *Daily Texan* in 1933.

During her extended year at the university, she took other measures to ensure that she would not have to return to Karnack or to become a teacher. She studied shorthand and typing so that she could go into business. She took those courses, she said years later, so that she had "the tools that can get you inside the door. Then, with a little skill and a great deal of industry, you can go on and take over the business — or else marry the boss!"

In June 1934 she earned a bachelor of journalism degree, again with honors. She did not seek immediate employment but went home to Karnack to supervise the redecoration of Brick House and spend time with her father and Aunt Effie.

The restoration of Brick House would take several months as it was rapidly deteriorating. When she was questioned about taking on the task, she explained that Mr. Taylor did not complain about anything she wanted. It was just that her father's idea of fixing up the house was to send Jack Moore, who worked at the store, with a bucket of white paint to paint something. The red bricks that had been made on the property were beginning to decay because of the moisture in the swampy area. The house was sanded and painted white to seal the bricks.

The task would require several trips between Karnack and Austin or Dallas for materials. After that she intended to use her skills in finding employment. Her first choice was to become a drama critic on a newspaper, but she would use her teaching certificate if that failed. She might even go away as far as "Hawaii or Alaska" if she could get a job.

As a graduation gift, her father gave her a trip to the eastern United States. Gene Boehringer asked her to look up her friend Lyndon Johnson, who she said was "just the brightest young man. He knows everything about Washington. I'm going to write him that you're coming, and here's his name and address and telephone number, and you call him!"

Lady Bird took the information and filed it away in her purse. She went to New York by boat and to the capital by train, but she did not call on Lyndon Johnson. "I was having a good time," she said, "and I just hesitated to call somebody I didn't know." She had not overcome her shyness in five years at the University of Texas.

Lady Bird had taken advantage of her university years, but if in those years she found "all the doors of the world suddenly were swung open" to her, she was referring just to the intellectual world. She was not referring to the emotional world she would soon discover in Lyndon Baines Johnson. When she finally met him in September 1934, her immediate reaction was: "I knew I had met something quite remarkable, but I didn't quite know what."

Lady Bird had gone to Austin to check on some materials for the redecoration of Brick House in the fall of 1934. She visited her friend Gene Boehringer, who was still working for C. V. Terrell, chairman of the Texas Railroad Commission. Terrell was bus inspector Sam Johnson's boss, and Sam had introduced the vivacious, pretty young woman to his son Lyndon. Lyndon had asked Gene for a date and was refused. But the two became friends and often went places together when Lyndon was in Austin.

In September 1934, Lyndon, Congressman Richard

Kleberg's secretary, was passing through Austin on his way back to Washington and had asked Gene to get him a blind date for the evening. She arranged a date with Dorothy McElroy, who also worked in Terrell's office. That afternoon Lady Bird dropped by to talk to Gene and was there when Lyndon arrived to see Gene.

Gene had already talked about Lady Bird to Lyndon, so he knew who she was. He invited Gene, Dorothy, and Lady Bird to go with him for a drink after work that day. While they were out, he quietly asked her to meet him for breakfast the next morning in the coffee shop of the Driskill Hotel. She reluctantly accepted. "I was uncertain whether I wanted to have breakfast with him, as I had a queer sort of moth-and-the-flame feeling about what a remarkable man he was."

On her way to see the architect Hugo Kuehne about remodeling Brick House, Lady Bird had to pass by the Driskill Hotel the next morning. Kuehne's office was next door to the coffee shop. She did not plan to meet Lyndon, but as she passed the coffee shop, he was sitting in the window. When he saw her passing and realized that she did not intend to come in, he frantically waved at her until she joined him in the shop. She said later, "I dare say I was going all the time, but just telling myself I wasn't going."

Lady Bird was twenty-one and Lyndon Johnson was twenty-six when they met. She found him "excessively thin but very, very good-looking with lots of hair, quite black and wavy." He was "terribly, terribly interesting" and "the most outspoken, straight-forward, determined young man I had ever met."

The most "determined young man" that Lady Bird had ever met was characterized by a "mind set" by all who knew him. Once he decided on something, he would not let go until he achieved his goal. On that first meeting, he decided he would marry Claudia Alta (Lady Bird) Taylor.

CHAPTER 3

Lyndon Baines Johnson

Hubert H. Humphrey, vice-president of the United States from 1964 to 1968, said of Lyndon Baines Johnson: ". . . above all he was a man steeped in politics. Politics was not an avocation with him. It was it. It was *the* vocation. It was his life. It was his religion. It was his family. It was his social economic life. It was his totality."

Lyndon Baines Johnson was born in the west room of a small, frame farmhouse on the Pedernales River near Stonewall, Texas. He arrived during "the biggest storm" of the season at daybreak on August 27, 1908. His parents were Sam Ealy, Jr., and Rebekah Baines Johnson. Lyndon, the oldest of five children, had one brother, Sam Houston, and three sisters, Rebekah, Josefa, and Lucia.

His mother had attended two years at Baylor University, where her father had been president of the college, and taught elocution to private students who could afford the tuition. Her specialty was public speaking and drama. It was known and accepted among the family that Lyndon was her favorite child. She pinned all her hopes and dreams on his success in politics. She was a strong, determined woman. She had given up what she believed to be a career in journalism to marry Sam Ealy, Jr. She was disappointed in her husband and transferred her dreams of political success to their first-born, Lyndon.

Some writers have stated that Rebekah was the greatest influence on her oldest child's life, but family members have said that Sam Ealy, Jr., was the major force in shaping Lyndon for politics. Sam Ealy, a Democrat, was first elected to the state legislature at the age of twenty-seven and served several terms. He supported bills regulating the employment of women and minors, fixing a minimum wage for them. He helped pass many laws that protected the poor from "wholesale swindling."

Ava Johnson Cox, a cousin two years or so older than Lyndon and affectionately called Sister by the family, said, "Sam Ealy was the one to encourage learning, speaking, and debate among the young ones.

"Every week-end when he came home from Austin, he brought books that he had checked out of the Extension Loan Library at the University of Texas. He gave us assignments to learn by the end of the next week when he returned. He lined us up in front of the hearth and questioned us as fast as we could answer. If he asked us something that we didn't know the answer to, you better believe, we knew it the next week-end when he came home.

"He divided us into debate teams. 'Now you three take the negative and you three take the affirmative.' The League of Nations was forming during that time and we had to debate the issue. Sometimes one group would be Democrats, one Republicans and one Socialists. And we had to know what we were talking about!"

Sam Ealy also taught them math by using dominoes. They had contests to see who could call out the correct number of dots on a domino as he turned them over. They practiced their multiplication tables and addition in this way, as well as competing in games. In fact, most of the things Sam Ealy taught the children was by competition in some way.

Lyndon signed this photograph for Lady Bird in 1934, before they became engaged.

— Courtesy LBJ Library

One of his favorite sayings was, "You better eyeball the person you are speaking to and know what you are saying." Lyndon used this to his advantage in later years when he was campaigning for office himself.

Sam Ealy Johnson, Jr., loved politics. He is credited with the beginning of the decline of the Ku Klux Klan in Texas by his speech to the House of Representatives deploring the bigotry of the group. Wright Patman wrote a bill and presented it to the legislature that made wearing a mask a prison offense. The East Texas Klan threw rocks and broke the windows in Patman's house. The Johnson family was afraid Sam Ealy would be "tarred and feathered." After Sam's speech, he and two of his brothers stood on their porch with shotguns and watched all night but no one came. Even though his life was threatened by the group, he stood by his attack, which had an influence on Lyndon's future Civil Rights Bill as president of the United States.

Sam Ealy could not support his family of five children on the $5 per day paid by the state legislature during regular session and $2 per day for extensions. During the early years he was in politics, a person could run for state office for a two-year term every other two years. He served two years and then was replaced by someone else the next term of two years. Unfortunately, he began drinking alcohol excessively. He tried farming, ranching, and real estate before he died in poverty in 1937. Lyndon eventually paid off all of his father's debts, including the cost of the funeral.

The Johnson family was involved in politics from the grandfather Sam Johnson, Sr., through his son Sam Ealy and his son-in-law Clarence Martin, who had beaten Sam, Sr., in a race for the legislature. While there were political differences in the family, they had a close family relationship. Each Christmas the family gathered at the Clarence Martin home, which was the most impressive of the Johnson clan. The children had to stand on a two-

and-a-half-foot raised hearth and recite an original work before they could open their gifts.

Elementary school for the Johnson children was split between the Junction school near Stonewall and Johnson City, depending on what Sam Ealy was doing at the time. Lyndon began going to school when he was four because he already knew how to read. Even though he learned to read at a very early age, reading was never a favorite pastime for him. His mother often followed him out of the house reading his assignment to him before he left for school.

Transportation to school was by donkey when they were in Stonewall. Those who had donkeys offered rides to some who walked. The donkeys were tied in the school playground during the day and watered at lunchtime. Lyndon began horseback riding when he was still in diapers. He often rode behind his cousin Ava across fields and the river to deliver mail to their grandfather's house. No one worried when he began riding to school behind someone on a donkey. Sam Ealy kept horses on the Johnson ranch but kept only the ones he considered Democrats. The Republican ones, the ones which balked in the mud, were quickly sold to someone else.

Textbooks had to be bought during that time and were used by many children in the family. Cloth book covers were made from old aprons or skirts to protect the books from dirty hands. No one was allowed to "dog-ear" or mark in the books. When everyone in the family used the books, they were sold back to the school or sold at a reduced price to cousins or neighbors.

Lyndon grew up like any other youth in the Stonewall-Johnson City area of the 1920s. The Johnsons were no poorer than their neighbors. They did not think of themselves as being poor during the time because almost everyone else was in the same situation. Lyndon earned money in as many different ways as the other boys and girls his age. Sometimes he picked cotton, although that was his least favorite way of earning money. At one time he had his own shoeshine business in the local barber shop. There he listened, learned, and enjoyed the talk about politics. He also worked on ranches and farms. When his dog had pups, he put a sign on the front gate of the house: "See me first for hound pups." He sold all of them.

The young people did not date separately but went places in groups. No one had much money or transportation. They chipped in ten cents per person and rented an old flatbed truck to take them to Stonewall or Blanco or surrounding areas for ballgames and different activities. There were few automobiles in the community — only three sedans, and the rest were open roadsters. The girls sang: "I don't like the kind of man/Who does his loving in a Ford sedan!"

The young people swam in the Pedernales River in cut-off overalls and worn-out denim shirts. When they found a chicken that had "strayed" from its pen, they had a picnic by the river. They went to ballgames, church meetings, and ice-cream socials. There were no radios or televisions to entertain them, so they became a competitive group who tried to outdo each other with ideas.

Lyndon graduated from Johnson City High School in 1924, when he was fifteen years old. He is said to be the youngest graduate in the history of the high school. He delivered the class poem and prophecy: "Give the world the best you have and the best will come back to you."

Lyndon was already six feet three inches tall, and his classmates considered him a leader. The class prediction was that he would become governor of Texas. While he may have had that ambition, he did not express it at the time. He was very young to graduate from high school; and, much to his mother's dismay, he told his family that he was "through with going to school" after graduation.

He did odd jobs in Robstown, Texas, for a short time. He and four young men from the Hill Country pooled their money to buy a Model-T Ford, which they drove to

California to find work. O. P. Summy, one of the young men, said about the trip, "We lived entirely on fatback and bacon, cornbread and homemade molasses." With little provision for trouble, the group made the trip in eight days with only one flat when they arrived at San Bernardino.

Lyndon left the group in San Bernardino but could not find a good job. "I had several jobs, but didn't hold any of them for long. I washed a few cars. I hashed in a cafe. I'd say, 'Shipwreck, two, please.' That means scrambled, two eggs," he later recalled.

He returned home when he became homesick and discouraged about making his fortune. For two years he wandered from job to job before he decided to go to college. He worked on a road gang for the highway department and found that he did not want to spend his life drifting from one manual labor job to another.

Lyndon decided to go to Southwest Texas State Teachers College in San Marcos, Texas. He had to borrow the money to enroll. Tuition was $17 a term (semester), which included books. He found that he was ineligible to attend because Johnson City High School was not a state-accredited school. Before he could get credit for course work or work on a degree, he had to take a six-week subcollege course and pass an examination to be officially admitted to the college. His mother moved to San Marcos and tutored him for six weeks. Even with the hard work, he barely managed to pass the exam.

He earned his college expenses by working in the office of the college president. At the end of his sophomore year, he left college to become a teacher and principal at a grade school for one year at Cotulla, Texas, beginning in September 1928. He completed some college course requirements by correspondence during the year he was teaching and returned to San Marcos to complete his senior year. In August 1930, he graduated with a bachelor of science degree.

Cotulla community consisted primarily of Mexican-

Americans. Many of the pupils were hungry and not properly clothed, and they were not interested in school and organized activities. Lyndon organized basketball and baseball teams as well as taught in the grade school. As principal of the grade school, he had authority over the other teachers. Before he went to Cotulla, there was no supervision of the children on the playground at recess and lunch. He required the teachers to begin supervising organized activities. They rebelled and threatened to quit. When he was told by the school board that he could replace the teachers if they did not cooperate, the teachers grudgingly began the duties.

His Cotulla experience influenced his life-long interest in education. He later said, "Somehow you never forget what poverty and hatred can do when you see its scars on the hopeful face of a young child."

The year in Cotulla was not all work and study. Lyndon fell in love with "a pretty girl" while he was still a student at Southwest Texas. Much to his embarrassment, she had a teaching job that paid her more than he earned. She lived thirty-five miles from Cotulla and taught civics and American history. He said, "She didn't know a thing about either. Never heard of a county judge, but was an expert in Spanish." Lyndon needed help in Spanish. He wrote her lesson plans and tried to teach her "the difference between a governor and a president" in exchange for Spanish lessons. He later said he did learn to say *"Buenos tardes, amigos"* between going to the movies and courting.

Lyndon was offered a renewed contract in Cotulla, but he decided to return to San Marcos to complete his degree. His favorite college instructor, Professor Greene, taught government and debate. Lyndon excelled in both. After he received his degree, he was debate coach at Sam Houston High School in Houston, where he was very successful. Luther E. Jones, Jr., a former debate student of Lyndon's, said "he was characterized by enormous physical energy. In fact, all the qualities that people associated with him as president were manifested at this early period . . . For the 'Chief,' as I and others came to call him, had already decided he would make state champions of us." The debate team ended second in the state debate competitions that year.

In 1931, the summer after his year as a debate coach, Lyndon made his first political speech. He was at a political rally where Pat Neff, a former governor, was up for reelection to the Texas Railroad Commission. The master of ceremonies called two or three times for Pat Neff to speak or for someone to speak for him. Just as he was about to pass on to the next speaker, Lyndon came pushing through the crowd, black hair flying and long arms waving, yelling, "By God, I'll make a speech for Pat Neff." He climbed upon the tailgate of a truck and made a ten-minute tribute to Pat Neff. When Welly K. Hopkins, who was running for the state senate, asked him why he did it, he replied, "Governor Neff once gave my daddy a job when he needed it, so I couldn't let him go by default."

Hopkins and Lyndon became friends in a very short time. Hopkins asked Lyndon to run his campaign for state senator in Blanco and Hays counties. Lyndon ran them and, according to Hopkins, "did a magnificent job." Hopkins was instrumental in getting Lyndon his first Washington job as secretary to Congressman Richard Kleberg, one of the heirs to the King Ranch.

The King Ranch and the Klebergs were not unknown to Lyndon. His father's brother Tom had been tick eradication control officer and had worked with Richard Kleberg on the King Ranch. Kleberg was one of the first ranchers to become interested in and supportive of the state's tick eradication program. Ava, Tom's daughter and Lyndon's favorite cousin, often accompanied her father on trips to open ranch gates for him. Ava and Lyndon were friends as well as cousins, and he sometimes went with them. When the foreman of King Ranch asked who the boy was with them, Ava quickly replied, "He's my little brother." She said, "Lyndon was always inquisitive and he not only observed what was going on, he asked questions as fast as they could be answered. He looked, listened, and learned. He loved ranching at an early age."

When Richard Kleberg filled the position in Congress left open by the untimely death of Congressman Harry M. Wurzbach, Welly K. Hopkins as well as others recommended Lyndon as his personal secretary (administrative assistant). Lyndon went to Corpus Christi for the job interview. He was debate coach again that fall at Sam Houston High School when he received the telephone call at school that he had the job. His principal released him from his school contract to accept the Washington position.

After working in Kleberg's Corpus Christi office for several weeks, Lyndon made his first train trip outside of Texas. He remembered thinking that the Capitol dome which seemed only a few steps away from the Union Station was a place he had "every intention of being one day as a congressman in my own right."

Lyndon lived in the sub-basement rooms of the Dodge Hotel, which was within walking distance of the Capitol and the Senate and House office buildings. Several of the secretaries of members of the House and Senate lived there. The rooms were not luxurious by any standards, but they were inexpensive. The young men spent very little time in the rooms except to sleep. Lyndon frequently led their many lively discussions. He often took positions that he didn't really support just to see how his colleagues would react. He was an eternal debater, and the subject was always politics.

The secretaries formed a group they named "The Little Congress." Lyndon was elected speaker of the group and represented them at a convention in New York. Several of the young men took the train to New York for a weekend of fun. Lyndon took his job more seriously than his friends did and spent most of the time trying to convince other delegates to the convention to think like he did.

For two and one half years Lyndon ran Kleberg's office force as well as the man himself. For all practical purposes, Lyndon was the congressman for Kleberg's office. It was on a trip to Texas to take care of Kleberg's business in September 1934 that he met Claudia Alta Taylor through their mutual friend Gene Boehringer in Austin.

Shortly after meeting Lady Bird, Lyndon enrolled in Georgetown Law School. He turned over the running of Kleberg's office to his brother, Sam Houston. He disliked law school because it seemed the professor only went over material he had just learned in homework. "He's not telling me anything I don't know," he'd mutter to Luther Jones, who sat beside him in class. After three weeks he dropped out and later joked that he "earned a B.A. degree — for Brief Attendance!"

He may have quit law school, but he pursued Lady Bird with the same energy he displayed in anything he decided to do. He decided immediately that he wanted her for his wife and proposed to her on their first date. When she was asked what she thought when he proposed, Lady Bird said, "It would be hard to say what I thought. I was just astonished, amazed. It was just like finding yourself in the middle of a whirlwind. I just had not met up with that kind of vitality before. I wanted to stay off on the edges of it. I wasn't sure I wanted to get caught up in it as a matter of self-preservation."

Lyndon said when he met Lady Bird he decided immediately "to keep her mind completely on me until the moment I had to leave for Washington four days later." Not being one to sit back and wait for things to happen, he did exactly that.

CHAPTER 4

Marriage

Lyndon Baines Johnson was the total opposite of soft-spoken Claudia Alta Taylor. He broke all the rules of reticence. On their first date, the day after they officially met through their mutual friend Gene Boehringer, he told her about his job, his family, and his ambitions. He asked her about her family, her education, her ambitions. "He also was telling me all sorts of things I would *never* have asked him, certainly [not] on the first acquaintance," she said.

They spent the day riding all over the countryside in a Ford roadster convertible with leather seats that had the King Ranch brand stamped into them. "He was rather gallant," Lady Bird said, "but he was a salesman through and through. But he was also very fair."

On the drive, he showered her with questions. "I never heard so many questions; he really wanted to find out all about me." Then Lyndon whose "mind could follow another mind around and get there before it did" gave her answers to "questions that hadn't been asked.

He told me all sorts of things I thought were extraordinarily direct for a first conversation."

He told her of his ambition to be in politics and how determined he was to become somebody. He was already well on his way as secretary to Congressman Richard Kleberg of the King Ranch dynasty. He told her what his salary was and how much insurance he had. He told her about his family. "It was just as if he was ready to give me a picture of his life and what he might be capable of doing," Lady Bird recalled.

When Lyndon proposed marriage to Lady Bird on their first date, she said, "I thought it was some kind of joke."

"Listen, you're seeing the best side of me. I'm trying to, but I think you ought to know that," he told her.

She was impressed and he was insistent.

The next day he took her to San Marcos to meet his parents, Sam and Rebekah Johnson, and spoke as if she were already a family member. The older Johnsons had moved to San Marcos so that their other children could go to college. It was less expensive for the children to live at home, and since the Johnsons did not own a home, it was easy for the whole family to move.

Lady Bird described her first meeting with Lyndon's father: "I felt sorry for him. It was obvious that he had been a vigorous, roaring personality once. Now he had a job — a poor-paying one — only because someone remembered him from back when. He was an old and ill man, old and ill before his time."

She found Rebekah Johnson to be "a lady." Lady Bird said, "It was obvious that Lyndon just loved her greatly, and I felt drawn to her, and yet I felt like patting her on the shoulder and saying I wasn't going to harm this son on whom she had pinned so many hopes. I just felt like saying, 'Don't you worry.' I had no intention at that time of getting married.

"The house was extremely modest. It was obvious that she had done what she could to make it prettier, had

The new Mr. and Mrs. Lyndon B. Johnson, on their honeymoon.
— Courtesy LBJ Library

bought some furniture and nice bedspreads, but it was extremely modest. Lyndon knew it, and knew I knew it, and was kind of watching me look at it. But he was intensely proud of his family."

On the third day of their acquaintance, Lyndon took her to the King Ranch, home of Congressman Kleberg. She was very impressed by the feudal empire surrounding Kingsville. She told her friends that it was so big that the Klebergs and their retainers used compasses the way other men used watches. He introduced her to the entire Kleberg family and told them he had asked her to marry him. Grandma Kleberg took her aside and told her that Lyndon was a fine young man and that she should marry him.

A week after they met, Lyndon had to leave for Washington. Lady Bird invited him and his traveling companion, Malcolm Bardwell, Congressman Maury Maverick's secretary, to stop over for a night at Brick House, which was on their way. Lyndon drove Lady Bird in her car and Bardwell followed. He did not want to miss an opportunity to keep Lady Bird's mind on him.

Lyndon was nervous about the impression he would make on her and her father. He exploded with embarrassment the morning after they arrived, when Bardwell appeared downstairs in his pajamas. He told Bardwell, "I'm going to marry this girl. You're going to ruin my marriage if you run around this way."

Lady Bird's father liked Lyndon from the first meeting. They were much alike. Both were big men physically. Lady Bird remarked to a college friend, "He is the only man I've ever met who is taller than my daddy." Both were work-minded and always in a hurry. Lady Bird later said, "I could tell that Daddy was right impressed with him." After dinner, he told her in a quiet moment, "Daughter, you've been bringing home a lot of boys. This time, you've brought a man."

Lyndon again asked her to marry him before he drove away toward Washington. She shyly refused his proposal but did kiss him before they parted. The story has been told that a neighbor witnessed the kiss and shouted at Lyndon, "Don't do that! Hurry up, go on or the Ku Klux Klan will get you!"

Lady Bird expressed her confused state of emotions to friends after Lyndon was gone. She had never felt that way before about any young man. She didn't know him well enough to marry him, although he had crammed his life's history into one week. She felt he was unusual, but there was also a little fear of getting caught up in his energy and ambition. She found him "a little bit scary — so dynamic and so insistent." Even though she was drawn to him, her "instinct was to withdraw."

When Lyndon arrived back in Washington, Gene Latimer and Luther Jones, friends and assistants in Kleberg's office, saw the surest possible sign that Lyndon's intentions were serious toward Lady Bird. His morning routine had always been inflexible, and he "always had this invariable rhythm" which nothing had ever been permitted to interrupt. After meeting Lady Bird, "he would go into Kleberg's private office, shutting the door behind him and sitting down to compose a daily letter to this young woman with the funny nickname whom he had met down in Austin." Latimer, who worked for Lyndon many years, said that during the early years of his career "that was the only time he [Lyndon] ever got out of that rhythm — that one time, getting off that letter to Bird. The one and only time."

Lyndon took a lot of care writing the letters to Lady Bird. He considered Gene Latimer to be a brilliant letter writer. When he finished a draft of a letter, he asked Gene to make corrections in "the spelling and should there be a comma, or was that a dangling participle. He'd say, 'You know, Bird's got a journalism degree.'"

Lyndon pushed for an answer to his marriage proposal in his letters just as persistently as he had in person. He assured her of his ambition in a letter dated October 24, 1934: "My dear Bird, This morning I'm ambitious, proud, energetic and very madly in love with you — I want to see people — want to walk thru' the throngs — want to do things with a drive . . ." He pressed her to say yes to his proposal: "I see something I *know* I want — I *immediately exert efforts* to get it — I do or I don't but I try and do my best . . . You see something you *might* want . . . You tear it to pieces in an effort to determine if you should want it . . . Then you . . . conclude that maybe the desire isn't an 'everlasting' one and that the 'sane thing to do is to wait a year or so'. . ."

He tried to convince her that they had mutual interests in cultural matters that were important to her. He wrote, "Every interesting place I see I make a mental reservation and tell myself that I shall take you there when you are mine. I want to go through the Museum, the Congressional Library, the Smithsonian, the Civil War battlefields and all of those most interesting places . . ." And he asked, "Why must we wait twelve long months to begin to do the things we want to do forever and ever?"

By this time, Lady Bird had accepted her nickname and wrote to Lyndon on personalized stationery with the name "Bird Taylor." She talked about the interests she believed they would eventually share: "Dearest: I've been reading *Early Autumn* [by Louis Bromfield] and am enthralled. If we were together, I'd read it to you . . . There's nothing I'd like better than being comfortable in a nice cozy place and reading something amusing or well-written or interesting, to someone I like. All good things are better shared, aren't they?"

She also told him about the flowers that she and her friend Dorris Powell saw as they had walked around Karnack. She continued her love of nature and her awareness of the landscape around her. About the old Haggerty place, she wrote, "There are the tallest magnolias I've ever seen, and great live oaks, and myriads of crepe myrtle, and a carpet of jonquils and flags in the spring."

She also responded to his personal concerns. "I would hate for you to go into politics," she told him, but then added immediately, "Don't let me get things any more muddled for you than they are though, dearest!"

While Lady Bird spent the days remodeling Brick House, a part of her mind was trying to decide whether or not to marry Lyndon. They wrote long letters and he telephoned almost daily although "you hear[d] about every third word, and so d[id] the eavesdropping neighbors." They steadily headed toward marriage.

Early in November, Lady Bird and Lyndon talked by telephone and decided that he would come from Washington and they would decide if they would become engaged. Less than twenty-four hours later, much to Lady Bird's shock, Lyndon came driving up the red-clay, rutted driveway to Brick House in a Model-A Ford roadster that he had purchased for $400. He had arrived at least a day before she was expecting him. "I hadn't gotten the house quite ready, and I hadn't been to the beauty parlor," she said.

"Let's go on and get married, not next year . . . but about two weeks from now, a month from now, or right away," he began arguing as soon as he arrived.

He was very persuasive, and she agreed to let him buy her an engagement ring. They left Karnack immediately and drove 300 miles to Austin to pick out a ring together. In the jewelry store they chose an engagement ring, and Lyndon wanted to buy a matching wedding band. Lady Bird refused to allow him to buy the wedding band. She also refused to make any decision about marriage without going to Alabama and talking to Aunt Effie. "She had concentrated all her life and all her love on me, and I just knew that I had to go and see her," she said later.

Lady Bird drove to Alabama while Lyndon drove to Corpus Christi to take care of some business for Congressman Kleberg. Aunt Effie was appalled that Lady Bird would even think about marrying a man she had known less than two months. She advised her to wait to get to know him better and assured her that it would be a mistake to rush into marriage when she had known him for such a short time.

When Lady Bird returned to Karnack, Lyndon's Ford roadster was already parked in the driveway of Brick House. She reported Aunt Effie's reaction and expressed her own doubts about a hasty marriage. Her father said, "If you wait until Aunt Effie is ready, you will never marry anyone," and added, "Some of the best deals are made in a hurry."

Lady Bird recalled later, "Sometimes in the course of the indecision I would get out the prayer book and look at the marriage service, which is actually a contract, and read it and decide, 'My gosh, I have changed so much in the five years I've been having dates — what if I had married one of those boys? That would have been disaster. I can't promise to love somebody forever; I might change.' Well, finally I decided that although one did change, one made the decision and went forward with hope."

The decision to marry was not an easy one to make and again she delayed making it. On November 17, 1934, she said she wanted to ask Gene Boehringer's advice. Lyndon insisted on driving her back to Austin himself. They had barely started the drive when he issued an ultimatum: "We either get married now or we never will. And if you say goodbye to me, it just proves to me that you just don't love me enough to dare to. And I just can't bear to go on and keep wondering if it will ever happen." She agreed to get married at once in spite of all her doubts. Lyndon let out a "Texas yip" that Lady Bird "was sure could be heard in the next county."

The engagement was a short one. It lasted only as long as it took them to drive from Karnack to San Antonio. Lyndon took no chances on making arrangements for the marriage in San Antonio on such short notice. He called his friend, Postmaster Dan Quill, who had some influence at City Hall. Quill was able to rush through an immediate marriage license. He contacted an Episcopalian minister, Reverend Arthur R. McKinstry of St. Mark's Episcopal Church, to perform the ceremony.

Reverend McKinstry refused to marry two people he had never met on such short notice. He declared it would be a "justice-of-the-peace ceremony." He preferred to counsel with young people before they were married so that he could feel certain that he was doing the right thing by performing the ceremony in the church. Quill convinced him that he would be doing the correct thing in marrying Claudia Alta Taylor and Lyndon Baines Johnson that evening. The minister reluctantly agreed to do it.

Dan Quill had reserved a room for them at the Plaza Hotel and waited for them there. After they had dressed for the wedding, both in informal clothes, Lady Bird asked Dan Quill about the wedding ring. Although Quill was irritated that they had driven past many jewelry stores on the way to San Antonio without getting a ring, he ran across the street to Sears-Roebuck Company. When the salesperson asked what size, he didn't know. He took about a dozen gold wedding bands on a stick to the hotel. Lady Bird tried on rings until one fit. Quill returned the extra rings and paid $2.50 for the one she kept. Many years later he joked about buying the ring and never being paid for it.

Lyndon said that as he and Lady Bird walked into St. Mark's Episcopal Church, he was still persuading Lady Bird that she was doing the right thing. Quill pushed Henry Hirschberg forward to act as a witness with Cecille Harrison, Lady Bird's former university roommate. Hirschberg's wife and Quill had called several people and invited them to the wedding.

The ceremony was short and simple. As they left the church to celebrate the wedding, Reverend McKinstry was heard to mutter, "This marriage won't last!"

Mrs. Hirschberg made reservations at the St. Anthony's Hotel Roof Garden for a wedding supper when she learned that nothing had been planned to celebrate the wedding. Liquor was not allowed in the hotel restaurant but Hirschberg, who was a lawyer, sent his brother-in-law to their house "to get a couple of bottles of sparkling burgundy." Hirschberg was a well-known St. Anthony's customer, so the management "looked the other way" while the small party toasted the newly married couple. Lady Bird was toasting her own wedding before she had time to think or change her mind.

The newlyweds left for the Plaza Hotel to spend their wedding night before taking a short honeymoon trip to Mexico. The next morning, Lyndon called his parents in San Marcos and told them he was married. Lady Bird called her father and Gene Boehringer, who had been expecting her in Austin, and said, "Lyndon and I committed matrimony last night."

The hasty marriage that Reverend McKinstry predicted "won't last" spanned over four decades, until the death of Lyndon Baines Johnson.

CHAPTER 5

Early Washington Years

Quiet, retiring Lady Bird Taylor had not been trained for marriage to Lyndon Baines Johnson. Most of her life had been spent alone with her father and Aunt Effie. She had been protected in a world of comfort and cared for by loyal black servants. Her marriage opened a door to a stream of new people and a world of constant activity. The world to which Lyndon introduced her was also one in which she was exposed to public scrutiny. Her new world brought loyal new friends as well as criticism. She had to learn to temper her soft, cultured ways with Lyndon's loud, aggressive and often earthy personality. The transition was not an easy or painless one for her.

From their honeymoon in Mexico they went to Washington, where they lived for a few days in an upstairs room at the Dodge Hotel where Lyndon had lived. Their first apartment was at 1910 Kalorama Road. It was a furnished, one-bedroom apartment with a small kitchen and living room.

Upon moving to the new apartment, Lyndon informed Lady Bird that he "wanted coffee in bed each

Lady Bird during 1941 Senate Campaign.
— Courtesy LBJ Library

morning." Lady Bird said she thought, "What!!! But I soon realized that it's less trouble serving someone that way than by setting the table and all." She took his newspaper to him in bed so he could read it while he sipped his coffee. She laid out his clothes and even placed things in the proper pockets that he would need during the day: a filled pen, cigarette lighter, handkerchief, and money. She also shined his shoes and placed his tie on the doorknob of the outside door so he could grab it on his way out.

One chore that she had difficulty training herself for was entertaining. Hospitality was a strong political weapon, and Lyndon used it to his advantage. They had barely settled into their new apartment when Lyndon informed Lady Bird that they were having guests for dinner, Congressman and Mrs. Maury Maverick.

Lady Bird's upbringing in a houseful of servants had not prepared her to cook for guests. Until the day they moved into the apartment, Lady Bird recalled, "I had never swept a floor, and I certainly had never cooked." When the Mavericks arrived for dinner, Lady Bird had set a small table in the living room. Mrs. Maverick said upon meeting Lady Bird, she felt "as if a little girl had invited me. One of the first things I saw was a Fannie Farmer cookbook open on the table. Staring at me was a recipe for boiled rice. The menu included baked ham, lemon pie and, of course, the rice. The ham and pie were very good, but I'll never forget that rice. It tasted like library paste. To this day, I connect boiled rice and library paste."

Mrs. Maverick was aware of her hostess's nervousness and was impressed with her unwavering smile in spite of it. Her warmth and sincerity made both the congressman and his wife, who were much older than the Johnsons, feel at home in the tiny apartment. That first small dinner was the beginning of Lady Bird's unchallenged reputation as one of the top hostesses in Washington during her years there.

Many other congressmen as well as reporters accepted invitations made by the Johnsons. It was not unusual for Lyndon to tell Lady Bird, "Get the furniture insured for Friday night. I'm having a bunch of newspapermen out . . . we'll have a wild evening." Everyone who came to the Johnsons' apartment felt that Lady Bird really meant it when she said goodnight at the door with "Y'all come back real soon, hear now?" She had a remarkable ability to make everyone feel at home within a very short time. It proved to be one of the biggest boosts to her husband's political career.

One of the guests who visited the Johnsons' apartment more and more was a congressman who was as shy in his own way as Lady Bird was in hers. Sam Rayburn was a man who seldom visited anyone and never visited anyone regularly. But he visited the Johnsons so frequently that soon he was coming every Sunday for breakfast. He stayed longer and longer each Sunday, sitting in a straight, hard chair and telling stories of Texas. Lady Bird cleaned up the breakfast things while Lyndon and "Mr. Sam" read the Sunday paper.

Rayburn had "adopted" Lyndon when he first came to Washington as Congressman Kleberg's secretary and treated him as a son. He was soon as fond of Lady Bird as he was of Lyndon. Lyndon and "Mr. Sam" spent hours talking politics and telling stories. "He [Sam Rayburn] was a great storyteller," Lady Bird said. "He remembered Woodrow Wilson and all these other figures." Because of Lady Bird's warmth in welcoming him in their home, the Johnson family became the family that Sam Rayburn never had.

Lady Bird had other adjustments to make in her marriage. Her husband's promise to take her "through the Museum, the Congressional Library, the Smithsonian, the Civil War battlefields and all of those most interesting places" did not materialize after their marriage. Lyndon worked all day, every day, and she explored Washington alone. "I'd just walk and explore, because it was all so fresh and new," she remarked about the thrill of her discoveries.

Lyndon's life centered around his work and he seldom, if ever, accompanied Lady Bird to a movie, which she enjoyed. She purchased two tickets to the Theatre Guild's four-play season at the National Theatre. Lyndon took her to the door but did not attend. Russell Brown, one of Lyndon's assistants, escorted her to the Theatre Guild that season.

Her dreams of sitting quietly and sharing the joy of a good book with her husband were not fulfilled. He had no time for anything except news magazines or the *Congressional Record*. She tried to underline paragraphs in books she thought he should read. Even if the subject was politics or government, he did not look at the book for more than a minute or two. She followed him around the apartment while he dressed to read aloud to him.

Several times during their marriage Lyndon remarked to her, "You don't sell for what you're worth!" He tried to draw her out of herself and present the person he knew to others. People, particularly Texans, often remarked, "I don't know how she stands it" when they overheard him criticize her dress. Others criticized Lyndon, but Lady Bird gave him credit for making her aware of her physical appearance and enhancing her personality.

Lady Bird did not want anything to call attention to herself and continued to buy clothes in drab colors. If Lyndon disapproved of the clothes she was wearing, he would tell her so in front of others. She began to wear slim dresses and high-heeled, stylish shoes. She went to a make-up artist to learn to soften her features and emphasize her dark brown eyes. A hair stylist gave her a short, attractive haircut. Lyndon pushed her to exercise and lose weight.

She said, "He always expected me to look better than I did, which meant that I had to make up in grooming and buying clothes and taking exercises for what didn't come naturally. Sometimes I wanted to rebel against that . . . But every now and then I saw someone who was just my own age and I imagined that I looked younger and acted younger, and if I did, it was because I had done all the extra things to look and feel better."

Lady Bird also gave her husband credit for helping her to develop a more open personality. "I was a much less gregarious person, much less interested in people, less outgoing or willing to make contact with others before I began to live with Lyndon. He has made me realize that it is more fun to have your life touch the lives of a lot of people, and let them know you like them. So, if there have been any growth and broadening in my relationships, if I have any more friends, I must give him a lot of credit for that too."

Another chore that Lady Bird was assigned after their marriage was to budget their monthly income. Lyndon's salary as secretary to Kleberg was $267 a month. Lady Bird gave him $100 to pay the car payments and insurance and for any incidental spending money he needed for the month. With the remaining $167, she paid $65 monthly rent and all household expenses including food for entertainment. She managed to purchase an $18.75 government bond every month. Lyndon complained, "I couldn't get five cents out of her that I didn't deserve."

Lyndon was the leader in their marriage. His wishes and tastes dominated their household. Lady Bird carried out what he wanted with calm and fortitude. In the early months of their marriage, the Johnsons set the pattern of their lives together.

In August 1935, less than a year after their marriage, Lyndon was offered the job of administrator of the National Youth Administration (NYA).

"How would you like to live in Austin?" Lyndon asked Lady Bird when he was appointed to the position. She said it was as if he had asked, "How would you like to go to heaven?"

Franklin D. Roosevelt, president of the United

States, established the NYA to give students jobs to help them stay in school and to employ nonstudent youth in public works. Lyndon was appointed the state director for Texas. The youngest director, at the age of twenty-six, he soon established a reputation nationwide for his efforts to place more minority students, blacks and Mexican-Americans, than any other NYA state director. In fact, he placed more young people, both boys and girls, than any other NYA agency.

On his way to Austin, Lyndon left Lady Bird for a short time at her father's home at Karnack while he established his office and staff in Austin. He wrote her, "It was more difficult to leave you last night than I had anticipated. I have learned to lean on you so much . . . Never have I been so dependent on anyone — Never shall I expect so much of any other individual." Those prophetic words proved true during their lives together.

Their first Austin home was at 4 Happy Hollow Lane, half of a small two-family dwelling with a large back yard. It was in that back yard that much of the business of NYA was conducted late into the night. The NYA building on Congress Avenue had a rule that all lights had to be turned off at 10:00 each night. But Johnson, a work-a-holic, demanded as much of his employees as he demanded of himself and Lady Bird.

Lady Bird was not told in advance when her husband would be home or how many guests for dinner would accompany him. She cooked dinner for them no matter how late the hour or how many there were. She did it with a graciousness and a smile that made them feel at home. Usually the food was gobbled down during talk of work. The guests spent the rest of the evening or most of the night in the back yard, where Lady Bird served dessert before leaving them to their work. She began a lifetime of cheerfully feeding unannounced guests.

Lady Bird and Lyndon later moved to the home of Robert and Gladys Montgomery. Robert Montgomery had gone to work in the Department of Agriculture in

Washington. The house was located at 2808 San Pedro Street, near the university area. Lyndon was making $7,500 per year and Lady Bird added a full-time maid who had a bedroom in the garage. Aunt Effie came to live with them, and both Lady Bird and Aunt Effie enjoyed the back yard which sloped from the house to the edge of the property. It included a spring and a natural amphitheater bordered by bamboo. There were flower gardens at several different levels.

Luther Jones and Willard Deason had both moved from Washington to Austin to work at the NYA with Lyndon. They lived at the Montgomery house as part of the family. Luther Jones said, "I never saw Lady Bird upset or irritated regardless of how many she fed or what time it was. She always made us feel welcome."

During Lyndon's tenure as the director of NYA, he established roadside parks in Texas. He had been given little money to work with but he had the manpower. He proposed to state highway officials that the NYA would pay the salaries of 15,000 unskilled young men to build roadside parks if the highway department would furnish the materials and heavy equipment necessary for the job. The highway officials agreed.

The roads at that time were narrow and often muddy, with bar ditches on each side of the road and little or no shoulder. People who stopped for a break from driving were often hit from behind. A migrant family had recently been killed when they were sleeping under their car, which was hit by a truck in the darkness. Gladys Montgomery had the idea of "a little drive-off for trucks and migrants to pull off and sleep in safety." Lyndon talked over the idea with Lady Bird, and the "roadside parks" became the first statewide project of the NYA youths in Texas. Lady Bird's love of nature moved from her own back yard to statewide. It was just the beginning of her influence on the environment.

NYA furnished the labor and the highway department furnished the equipment. Lyndon persuaded farmers to give small plots of land along the roads. The youths cleared the brush, laid down curbed driveways, and built concrete picnic tables, barbecue pits, and steps mounted over the fences to offer people "a private restroom." Gladys Montgomery's idea spread across the country with Lyndon Johnson's NYA work as a model.

Lyndon drove himself and his men to accomplish what appeared to be impossible tasks. Ernest Morgan related a time when a long-awaited WPA (Works Progress Administration) list of young people who were eligible for NYA employment arrived late on a Friday afternoon. Lyndon told Jim Deason and Morgan that he wanted the 8,000 teenagers at work on Monday morning. Their first reaction was disbelief and then despair. The teenagers couldn't be contacted by mail over the weekend. Besides, the NYA had already found that many teenagers did not respond to letters. At that time, Morgan was supervising twenty youths who were working on a roadside park. Lyndon told him to divide up the 8,000 names among the twenty youths and have them make direct contacts to the homes.

Morgan brought the youths to the NYA office and spent most of Friday night dividing the names among them by streets. Saturday morning they all "hit the streets." Morgan said, "We didn't contact all of them, but on Monday morning, we had 5,600 of them down there, and we put them to work. That's the kind of assignments he'd give you — that would seem nearly impossible. But he taught you you could do them."

Young women profited from the NYA's work in Austin. The association bought old houses and made them livable. Most of the girls who were high school dropouts were unemployed. About the only jobs they could get were as domestic help. When a house was repaired, a housemother was installed with as many girls as could comfortably live there. The housemother taught them personal hygiene and trained them to be excellent housekeepers or encouraged them to get other training. As the girls became independent, they moved out to allow other unemployed girls to take their places.

Lady Bird said, "Not many things have ever meant so much to us as the NYA, brief though it was."

James P. Buchanan, congressman from the Tenth District, died of a heart attack in February 1937. Lyndon wanted to run in the special election in April to replace Buchanan. There were several problems, but the most pressing one was money. He did not have the funds to finance a political campaign. Lady Bird talked with Alvin J. Wirtz, one of her husband's mentors. She became convinced that Lyndon had a chance to win in the election. She called her father and arranged to obtain $10,000 of her share of her mother's estate. Her father immediately deposited the money into her bank account.

Lyndon went to talk to his father, Sam Ealy. According to Ava Johnson Cox, Lyndon's cousin, Sam told him, "Son, some folks are going to say that you are too young, and you have to convince them that you can do the job. Shake hands like a man. Put feeling into it, don't give them a cold fish to shake, and look them in the eye when you talk to them. And don't forget the old people. That poor, old woman sitting on that bench over there has the same number of votes as that young man driving a new car and wearing a new suit."

Custom during that time still did not allow for women to openly seek votes for their spouses or anyone else in political campaigns. Lady Bird supported Lyndon by "keeping the home fires burning." She could not convince him to rest and eat properly. He lost weight and looked haggard and gray. Two days before the election, he collapsed during a speech and was taken to the hospital. On election day, Lyndon was in the hospital with appendicitis. Lady Bird wanted to stay at the hospital with him, but he suggested that she occupy her time "by taking friends and kinfolks and homebound elderly citizens to the polls and telephoning." She did as he asked. Lyndon defeated his opponents, "and that ushered in a new chapter in our [the Johnsons'] lives."

During her husband's campaign for Congress, Lady Bird was pleasant and uncomplaining as she served hot meals to Lyndon and his aides at all hours of the night. The men who worked for him had come to accept a warm, welcoming smile at the door, no matter when they arrived. Occasionally, someone who didn't know her well suggested that Lady Bird might campaign. The suggestion that she might have to face an audience and speak brought such panic to her face that the suggestion was always quickly dropped. Few people knew that she had once prayed for smallpox so that she wouldn't have to speak at her high school graduation ceremony if she were one of the top two graduates. Years later, looking back on that first campaign, Lady Bird said, "My only regret is that I did not have the gumption to share in it."

After the election, an Austin women's organization held a reception in honor of the wife of the new congressman. Lady Bird was able to avoid making a speech at the party, but she could not avoid standing in a receiving line to greet those who attended. As she shook hands and chatted with the strangers filing by, the bright smile on her face was as rigid as if it had been cut in stone. Only her friends knew she had done it by extreme effort and will.

Lyndon did not take care of himself or follow the doctor's orders after his appendectomy. He ended up having to stay in the hospital for almost two weeks after the election. When he was released from the hospital, they went to Karnack to visit Cap'n Taylor to give Lyndon time to rest and recuperate. Lyndon left for Washington on May 11, and was sworn in as congressman of the Tenth District on May 13.

After Lady Bird arrived in Washington, they made friends with Aubrey Williams, whose big, rambling house was open to a lively group of government people. "Roll up your sleeves and remake America" was a phrase that had come about during Franklin D. Roosevelt's presidency. The people who believed they were doing that gathered together, and the conversations were abundant and exciting. Lady Bird said, "Conversations always got back to politics, but they all had a social-economic bent. There was always a goal to achieve, some sort of improvement in agriculture or welfare or building dams or education. Reform and improvement were considered highly possible, and they [Johnson's acquaintances] were the people who were going to do it."

For the next four years, the biggest and most important word in Lady Bird's vocabulary was "constituency, which one spelled in capitals — CONSTITUENCY!" Lyndon poured his energies into work for the Tenth District and into fulfilling his ambition for higher political office. Lady Bird took constituents from the Tenth District to all of the tourist attractions of Washington. Before she assisted the visitors, she read all of the information she could find on the various attractions so she could answer any questions asked. The visitors were often impressed as she talked to them in her soft, Southern accent. It was obvious that she was very knowledgeable and comfortable with that knowledge. She also spent "hours going to innumerable weddings, gatherings, and in the first year or so paying calls."

The Johnsons returned to Austin between congressional sessions. It was necessary for Lady Bird to fill the car with household possessions and drive back and forth at the start and finish of each session. She did not mind the drive between Austin and Washington because she had a fear of flying and generally became airsick. It was the packing and moving that she disliked. Lyndon often had to remain in Washington and flew to Austin later. When he did not drive with her, she was accompanied by the wife of one of his aides. Lady Bird said of those trips, "My idea of being rich was having enough linens and pots and pans to have a set in each place, and not have to lug them back and forth."

Lady Bird began to pay closer attention to her appearance. She had always felt "dumpy" and was able to lose the weight and keep it off. She was still shy to an extreme and insecure in her position as wife of a congressman. She listened to the arguments of her husband and his political friends, never offering an opinion or making a statement. If they mentioned books about certain subjects, she checked those books out of the public library and read them. Often, as she listened to conversations, she knew as much on the subject as anyone else. She made no comments that would call attention to herself or would show her knowledge.

There seems to be no question that the 1930s were difficult ones in the Johnsons' marriage. They wanted to have children. They were saddened and disappointed each time they lost a child in several miscarriages. Lyndon's father, Sam Ealy, died in the late fall of 1937, leaving over $5,000 in debts, which took Lyndon years to pay. They had to maintain a house in Austin year-round as well as rent an apartment in Washington when Congress was in session. They helped Rebekah Johnson financially by hiring a young woman to help her with housework and a yardman after Sam Ealy's death.

By 1941, when Lyndon ran for the Senate, Lady Bird went with him on the campaign trail. She recorded the pageantry of the campaign in home movies but still did no obvious campaigning herself. Although President Franklin D. Roosevelt endorsed Lyndon for the position, he lost to Governor W. Lee "Pappy" O'Daniel. A disappointed Lyndon returned to Washington to serve five more terms in the United States House of Representatives until 1948. Of the defeat, Lady Bird said, "I think the experience was good for him. I can't say that a solid diet of success is good for anybody."

Disappointment of the lost election was forgotten with the beginning of World War II. Soon after Pearl Harbor, Lyndon applied for active duty as a naval-reserve officer. Lady Bird took a giant step in personal growth when she became "substitute congressman" for Lyndon for the first six months of 1942.

CHAPTER 6

The Businesswoman

Pearl Harbor, December 7, 1941, changed the lives of all Americans. Congress declared war on December 8, the day after the Japanese bombed Pearl Harbor. The Senate race was forgotten when Lyndon went on active duty as a naval-reserve officer. In the next several months Lady Bird first assisted with the operation of his Washington office and gradually assumed the work he had done.

In January 1942, Lady Bird began work in Lyndon's congressional office with only two staff members. Mary Rather was Lyndon's secretary, and O. J. Weber was a twenty-one-year-old with only a few months' experience. Both John Connally and Walter Jenkins, Lyndon's assistants, were on active duty. Herbert Henderson, Lyndon's speechwriter, had died suddenly in October. With the exception of Mary Rather, Lady Bird had no experienced people to advise her. She took the work seriously and did not begin to exert her authority over the others until she learned what she needed to know. Under her warm exterior manner, the office staff soon recognized that her standard was just as high as her husband's. Much to the dismay of Mary and O. J., she requested they retype any letters with errors, however small.

"The office is so stimulating and interesting that I graduated myself from business school and now get down here about eight-thirty every morning and stay until our Lyndon Johnson quitting time — which is when everything is done," she wrote to Lyndon.

She dealt with many and varied problems: the status of the city slaughterhouse in Austin, the location of an Army Air Support Command there, and the impact of rationing and housing policies in the district. She continued Lyndon's policy of writing to constituents to congratulate them on weddings, graduations, or local honors, and provided news about heroism, wounds, and deaths to those families with relatives in the war. During those months, Lady Bird received a political education. She wrote to a friend that she had learned more in three months than in four years in college.

She became involved in deciding whether Lyndon should enter the Senate primary against O'Daniel, who was seeking a full six-year term. She believed that it was in her husband's best interest to try for reelection to the House, since she thought it unlikely that he would defeat the popular O'Daniel. She discussed the decision with friends of Lyndon's and they agreed. The same friends helped her secure the petitions that put the congressman on the primary ballot without opposition in the Tenth District.

Letters to Lyndon during that time show her energy and commitment to the work she had taken on. "Never do I seem to catch up!" she wrote. "There are always things left over to talk to you about." In return he urged her to "Write Write Long Long Letters" and told her that the men around him expressed their high opinion of her contribution: "She is doing a bang up good job and the people are beginning to realize it."

Nellie Connally and Lady Bird had been friends be-

Lady Bird and Lyndon Johnson.
— Courtesy LBJ Library

fore their husbands went to war. They had attended business school together in the fall of 1941, and Nellie took her husband John's place in the congressional office when he went on active duty in the navy. Lady Bird was not paid for her work during that time, and she cut back on living expenses. She rented hers and Lyndon's apartment for $100 monthly and shared one with Nellie for $60 per month.

"By the time the end of the day came, when I had shifted my mental gears so many times . . . I was utterly exhausted. I didn't even want to make an unimportant decision," Lady Bird later remarked about those months. She was glad for Nellie's company and a good friend to decide where and what they would eat. Nellie was also loyal and one with whom she could discuss her frustrations when things did not go right in the office. They shared the same worries and fears about their husbands' war activities.

It was a tense time, but Lady Bird never lost her sense of humor. "When I think of Lyndon's being captured by the Japs," she wrote to Emily Crow in May 1942, "I think of O. Henry's 'Ransom of Red Chief'." And of the long, work-filled days during his absence, she said, "It gave me a sense of, sort of reassurance about myself because I finally emerged thinking that — well, I could make a living for myself."

By mid-July of 1942, President Roosevelt ordered all government officials to return to Washington. Lady Bird described Lyndon's return in August as "the grandest day of my life."

Lady Bird assumed a more active role in her husband's career after her months of running Lyndon's office. Jonathan Daniels, an aide to the president, noted in his diary for October 10, 1942: "Lyndon Johnson's wife is the sharp-eyed type who looks at every piece of furniture in the house, knows its period and design — though sometimes she is wrong. She is confident that her husband is going places and in her head she is furnishing the mansions of his future."

At that particular time in 1942, Lady Bird was more interested in furnishing a home. They had lived in seven apartments in five years and she was tired of moving. She made the decision to buy a house and found one they both liked. With Lyndon's unopposed reelection to Congress and his obsession with politics, she felt justified in buying a permanent dwelling. She was receiving enough money from her inheritance to make a sizable down payment on the house she wanted.

Lyndon had irritated the owners by trying to badger them into lowering the price by $2,000. They were considering withdrawing from the sale. Lyndon and John B. Connally, Jr., were talking politics as usual when Lady Bird interrupted. She had tried to talk to Lyndon before, and he had just ignored her. With black eyes sparkling in anger, she stated, "I want that house! Every woman wants a home of her own. I've lived out of a suitcase ever since we've been married. I have no home to look forward to. I have no children to look forward to, and I have nothing to look forward to but another election!"

She stormed from the room before either of the startled men could speak. Lyndon turned to Connally and asked, "What should I do?" Connally's answer was, "I'd buy the house." Lady Bird got her house: a two-story, eight-room, white brick colonial with an attic and a basement just a few blocks from Connecticut Avenue.

Lyndon said only twice during the years he knew Lady Bird did he see her really express her anger. Once was before they were married. They were mounted on horseback when her horse backed up. He thought she did not know how to stop the horse. "I gave him a whack across the back. He leaped forward, almost unseating her, and she expressed herself to me pretty forcefully," he recalled with a chuckle. The second time was when she wanted the house and he seemed to be endangering the purchase.

There were times when Lady Bird showed her anger. She said afterward that she "felt silly and absolutely weak." But she added, "It is probably not wise always to control one's temper. I think it might be better to blow up sometimes." She preferred to be "calm and reasonable and try to make those around me calm, help them to be."

In addition to controlling her temper, Lady Bird believed to a great degree that she could control her health. Perhaps due to her Aunt Effie's psychosomatic illnesses, Lady Bird would not admit to being in pain. She lost three children by miscarriage, but she never complained or admitted her discomfort. The only indication of her pain was the sadness her friends detected in her expressive eyes. Once Lyndon returned from a trip to Europe and found her ill in bed. She assured him it was all right for him to go to the office. Five minutes after he left, she telephoned her doctor, who rushed her to the hospital and operated immediately. "If she has one fault, it is that she just will not admit pain," Lyndon said about her.

For a while after the Johnsons purchased their first home, Lady Bird found particular pleasure in her garden and yard. "The sunshine was so inviting that I spent a couple of more enthusiastic than useful hours digging in my flower garden." Eventually the garden became "quite a remarkable" one, covering a large space in the back yard with zinnias and peonies.

As she took friends and constituents to the Botanical Gardens, Lady Bird carefully noted the periods of each year when the cherry blossoms and tulips came out in Washington. When she drove back and forth from Washington to Texas, she also marked the changes in the landscape: the junkyards, the billboards, and the impact of development on natural beauty. She said, "I loved the trips across the country to Washington, and I never got too many of them." But gradually over the years, she realized "commercial civilization" was destroying the natural beauty that belonged to every American. At the time that realization was stored in her mind to surface again in the near future.

When Lyndon took over his office again and became immersed in politics, Lady Bird did not want to be just a political wife, living in her husband's shadow. He was still first priority, but she now realized she needed a personal challenge. Before she ran his congressional office for several months, she had ambitions and dreams but little self-confidence. She was not sure she could even support herself if necessary. But during those months of meeting the everyday challenges and problems, she acquired an assurance and experience that gave her an appetite for more.

By the fall of 1942, Lyndon took care of the office, and Lady Bird was delegated to the home and constituents. Since she had no children to occupy her time and mind, she began to make plans for a new challenge. She wanted a business of their own that might one day support them in case Lyndon decided to leave politics.

Lady Bird wanted to buy a newspaper. She had even picked a newspaper that she wanted in Texas, but it cost too much for her. She heard about a small radio station in Austin with dual ownership that was to be sold, and she looked into its potentials. About that time she received a portion of her mother's estate, which her father had been holding for her. Eventually she received around $67,000 from the inheritance, but at that time she got $21,000. She added a $10,000 loan from the bank with her own $21,000 and negotiated for the purchase of KTBC.

KTBC was a small, debt-ridden radio station in Austin that was losing nearly $2,000 a month. In February 1943, the Federal Communications Commission granted approval of the sale, and Lady Bird was in business. When questioned about the advisability of buying a very run-down station, she answered, "I had a degree in journalism and we knew a lot of folks in the business. It just held an attraction for us, and we thought it was a coming industry."

Lyndon told Lady Bird, "You have to go down there and take that place over." Had she known what she would find, she might have been more reluctant to do so. When she walked into the station, two blocks off Congress Avenue, she found "that the place was *real* dirty. I mean cobwebs on the windows and the floor was grimy." Employees remembered that she scrubbed the floor herself. When the place was clean to her satisfaction, or as clean as was possible in the condition of the quarters, she turned to the business itself.

She searched through all the ledgers, contracts, and operational reports to find why the station was losing money and how to stop it. Those documents were not strangers to her. From the time she was twelve years old her mother's bachelor brother, Claude Patillo, for whom she was named, had been preparing her for the Harvard School of Business. When she did not go to Harvard or major in business, he continued to tutor her in property management, bookkeeping, and business methods. He was preparing her as the sole heir to his Alabama property. In between visits to Alabama, he mailed her books which she read and discussed with him. She lived up to his expectations although he did not live to see her accomplishments. He died in 1941.

In Austin, Lady Bird worked long hours to learn about the operation of the radio station. At the time she bought it, the station had no network affiliation. It operated only in the daytime and had nine employees. She first studied the "bad debts" and soon found a clue to some problems. Many of the advertisers refused to pay because they were dissatisfied with the service they had gotten from the station. She went through the entire list of debtors and determined what was valid and what was inaccurate.

During the first weeks the office staff had to make deposits of funds received each day before checks could be written to pay expenses. When she had straightened out the books, she turned her attention to the employees. She evaluated each one for his contribution to the business and ability to do his job. She decided she needed a new manager and hired one, Jesse Kellam. Kellam had succeeded Lyndon as NYA director in Austin and was highly trusted and respected by Lady Bird. She stayed on and worked night and day for five months with the new manager.

In August, the station showed a small profit. From that time on, the profit chart showed an upward trend. She brought in new staff members and began paying off old bills and working through the accounts receivable. Lyndon had complained to a family friend in May that "the radio station is pulling me down for the third time." Lady Bird was pleased to boast to him that the station was "in the black in August to the tune of eighteen dollars."

The five months of constant work and pressure were difficult ones for Lady Bird. She and Lyndon had little time together. There were brief times when he flew to Austin or she flew to Washington. They were in constant contact by letters and telephone, but both were relieved when she could return to Washington.

When Lady Bird finally went home in August to stay, she was in great spirits over her success in putting the station in the black — even by such a small profit. But her greatest happiness was learning that she was pregnant. She stopped her travel and many activities because of her history of miscarriages. She still ran the radio station while in Washington.

She persuaded the Federal Communications Commission to grant KTBC the right to broadcast twenty-four hours a day and to increase its transmitting power to 1,000 watts. She also obtained network affiliation with the Columbia Broadcasting System (CBS). She received detailed weekly reports about the station's progress along with monthly budgets.

For years before she moved into the White House, she received a large manila envelope every Saturday morning. It contained a complete account of the week's activities of the Austin radio and television stations, the only ones in which she had a personal hand in the management. For a few hours after the envelope's arrival, she stepped out of her role as a Washington wife and became a Texas business executive.

Each salesman for the stations made a report to her. He listed every call he had made during the week, the sales pitch he gave the merchant, and the response he got. There was also a daily account showing the amount of money received for the time sold each day of the week. This she compared with the same period of the preceding month and the previous year. "It gives you a graph of how you are doing," Lady Bird explained, "but it makes no sense until you look on the other side of the sheet and see whether your expenses are rising or not. That margin to the business person is the real gauge to how well you are doing."

She paid attention to the smallest details of the station's operation. As new employees were added, she tried to get to know each one personally and evaluate the potential contribution they might make to the business. When anyone did a good job, including writing a good report, she was quick to praise. She was always thinking of little extras to make life easier, more enjoyable for her staff. After the Johnsons had purchased ranch land near Johnson City, she allowed the staff to spend free weekends and vacations at one of the ranch houses. If she happened to be at the LBJ Ranch at the time, she would drop in to see them and take them small gifts. When one of the employees had a new baby, she sent a check in the baby's name to start a bank account for the new arrival.

Her business associates attributed her success in part because she "makes people want to do their best and she inspires them toward this end." She was patient in listening to both sides of each question. When she had all the facts, she made decisions quickly. The same business associates reported that she was, on the business side, "any man's equal; she reads a balance sheet like most women examine a piece of cloth." However chauvinistic the statement was, she took it as a compliment to her business skills.

By 1945, the assets of the station for which she had paid $30,000 were listed at $78,000. Luck was in Lady Bird's favor when the Federal Communications Commission allotted television channels to Austin. The LBJ Company applied for and received Channel 7. The FCC gave Austin one very-high-frequency channel (VHF) and two ultra-high-frequency channels (UHF). Those were the early days of television, and no one knew whether the future of television lay in UHF or VHF stations. There was only one other Austin applicant who requested a UHF station. Lady Bird requested the VHF just on a guess. She guessed right because television sets were made to receive only VHF stations, and people did not buy converters to tune in the UHF channels.

Profits for the LBJ Company soared with both a television station and a radio outlet in Austin. The corporation began to buy into radio and television stations in other towns. By 1963, the LBJ Company owned sizable shares in stations in Waco and Bryan, Texas, and Ardmore, Oklahoma.

When Lady Bird became First Lady of the United States, she had to place her broadcasting properties in a trusteeship to allay any suspicion of conflict of interest. At that time (1963) the total worth of her broadcasting holdings was estimated to be over $5 million.

Her success as a businesswoman, she insisted, was not due to any extraordinary qualities as a businesswoman or a broadcaster on her part. It was due to using good judgment. "If you are able to use good judgment, that is half the battle," she said. "Then you must have good people around you and you must keep them. We are fortunate in that respect. Our employees have been with us for years."

When she moved into the White House and had to

give up her interest in the station and all other media holdings, she wrote Jesse Kellam her regret in having to end her formal connections with KTBC: "Trading in a twenty-two year love and work for the months that lie ahead brought a torrent of thoughts and emotions in its wake . . . How I shall miss the plans, the people — even the problems — the affiliates conventions, yes, even the thick Saturday morning reports, the Christmas party, and perhaps even more, the summer parties with everybody's children."

Lady Bird's talents as a businesswoman were recognized beyond her own family circle and business associates. She won two outstanding honors for her achievement and leadership in broadcasting. The first was a gold-framed salute from Theta Sigma Phe, honorary sorority for women in journalism, for Lady Bird's "professional endeavors in radio and journalism and for inspiring increased respect for women's capabilities both in this country and abroad." The American Women in Radio and Television (AWRT) awarded her a citation in 1963 "in appreciation of her contribution to the broadcasting industry as a distinguished executive mindful of her responsibilities to her community and to her stations." The same group made her honorary chairman of Project One of the Educational Foundations of AWRT. And in 1975, *Ladies Home Journal* named her Woman of the Year for Quality of Life.

No records are available to show how much Lady Bird's business sense was supported by her husband's political clout to make such an impressive impact on the media world. That they were a partnership is undeniable, but Lady Bird proved that she "can pick up a balance sheet and look at it with the same discernment another woman displays toward a piece of cloth."

CHAPTER 7

Lady Bird and Her Daughters

The 1940s brought many changes in Lady Bird's life. She once remarked that "the 40's were good years for me." She became self-confident in her ability to run her husband's office while he was serving in World War II. They bought their first home in Washington and she had launched a new business which was showing a profit for the first time. But more important than any of her other accomplishments was that she became a mother.

She returned to Washington in August 1943, feeling very pleased with herself. She had successfully launched a radio station, but she had a more important reason for happiness. She was pregnant again. For almost ten years the Johnsons had tried to have children. Lady Bird had conceived three times and each had ended in a miscarriage.

She was aware of the dangers of miscarriage. Her mother had died due to an infection after a fall that caused her to miscarry. She was determined not to let the past tragedy affect her desire to have children. For several months Lady Bird reduced her activities and closely

Portrait of President Lyndon Johnson and family, February 1966.

— Courtesy LBJ Library

followed the doctor's instructions. On March 19, 1944, their first daughter was born. "I wanted to name her Lady Bird," Lyndon said, "but her mother preferred Lynda Bird, and since she is the boss I had to compromise."

Lady Bird was critically ill in the summer of 1946 and lost a baby because of a tubal pregnancy. She was restricted in activities for several weeks. Her doctor said it would be risky for her to become pregnant again. A year later, however, on July 2, 1947, the Johnsons had their second daughter, Lucy Baines Johnson. (She changed the spelling of her name to "Luci" when she was sixteen.) Lyndon was careful to point out that all of the Johnson family had the same initials, LBJ. He later joked about giving their daughters the same initials as his and Lady Bird's: "[I]t's cheaper this way, because we can all use the same luggage."

While some may see Lynda and Luci's lives as a fairy tale, they did not choose to live their lives in public view.

They were not allowed a normal childhood of always having their parents around or living in one place for a long period of time. Because of their father's prominence in politics, they were often the center of newspaper stories to satisfy public curiosity.

Lady Bird tried to impress upon them that the news they generated was because of the importance of their father's job. She did not want them to feel important because of it. She assured them more than once that "It's the job that is important, not you and me."

She tried to balance her roles as a mother and wife with her own business interests. Her role as a wife always took precedence. She did not like leaving her daughters in others' care so much of the time, but she recognized the importance of her support in Lyndon's political career. They were members of the official Washington society and were in constant demand. Also, she had business obligations in Texas and in Alabama after Claude Patillo's death in 1941 and her Aunt Effie's death in 1947. She often whispered in her daughters' ears "Remember you are loved," when she had to say goodbye. She was hurt when she learned Lynda and Luci referred to themselves as "deprivileged children."

"That has been one of the costs," she said. "It is one of the bills you have to pay for the job your husband has." Nevertheless, the ties between parents and daughters were always very close.

During the latter part of the 1940s, Lady Bird became more involved with her husband's political career. In the 1946 primary campaign, Hardy Hollers, Lyndon's opponent for Congress, made a big issue of the Johnsons' finances. At a crucial point in the campaign there was talk about having Lady Bird make a speech on the radio refuting his accusations that she did not purchase the business with her own money. She lived in fear of having to make the speech, but it became unnecessary. Lyndon won the election two votes to one.

Two years later, in 1948, Lyndon ran against Coke

Stevenson in a Senate race. Lady Bird and Marietta Brooks organized the Women's Division and toured the state together, speaking to groups of women. One newspaper reported that Lady Bird was "an able vote-getter," although the reporter found her "a rather modest woman" who "used to even be on the shy side." A runoff election was held in August 1948. Lady Bird spent countless hours writing friends to convey "our deep appreciation for your faithful and untiring work in his behalf" and urging them to get out and vote.

The night before the election she drove from Austin to San Antonio to appear with Lyndon and make a speech. The car in which she was riding was involved in two accidents on the way. About one of the accidents, Lady Bird said, "All I could think of while we were turning over in the car was that I wished I had voted absentee ballot so my vote would count." She finally arrived in a borrowed dress, bruised and nervous to "make a fine speech." She returned to Austin the same night and spent election day telephoning voters. Lyndon won the election by a margin of eighty-seven votes.

The vote was contested, which kept the Johnsons in court and suspense until he was sworn in as a senator in January 1949. "The 1948 campaign was one that just didn't end," Lady Bird said. "It just went on and on."

Election to the Senate made Lyndon a national figure. But being married to a national figure was not the only impact on Lady Bird's life that year. Lyndon purchased the Clarence Martin ranch from his aunt. The 415-acre property was located on the Pedernales River between Johnson City and Fredericksburg and was in a "dilapidated condition." When Lady Bird saw it, she said, "I was aghast!" She asked Lyndon, "How can you do this to me?" The house had been the most impressive of the Johnson clan when Lyndon was growing up and he remembered Christmases spent there. His aunt had lived there for fifty years, but the property had decayed over the years that she was a widow.

Lyndon's enthusiasm and the beauty of the Hill Country soon overcame her doubts. She gradually began to get wrapped up in it herself. She had always loved living on the land, but that particular land was so different from what she had known in East Texas.

Lady Bird attacked the problem of the run-down condition of the house and land as she attacked other problems in her life. She analyzed the situation, made decisions about what needed to be done, and set about doing it. She redecorated the house and changed the landscape.

The original stone house had been built by Lyndon's great-grandfather. Over the years fear of the Indians had subsided, and frame additions had been added as the family grew. Lady Bird used colors in the house that suggested the land itself: vivid greens, corals, browns, yellows, and blues. Most of the furniture came from a furnished house that Lady Bird had bought in Washington. She preserved some things from her mother-in-law's house to create a warm, homey atmosphere throughout the home.

While she was redecorating the house, she was also working on the landscape of the 415 acres. She spread seventy-five pounds of bluebonnet seeds on both sides of the river and spread other wildflower seeds where she thought they would grow. She consulted seed dealers about the best time to plant and how to plant. She reported "very minimum results from the considerable amounts I have planted" and wondered "whether it's a lost cause to try to plant wildflower seeds in an area where either cattle or sheep occasionally graze."

Wildflowers were not the only problem of the ranch. In 1952, the Pedernales River flooded. Lady Bird was at the ranch with Lynda and Luci and was pregnant again. Lyndon tried to fly in to get them, but on takeoff the single-engine airplane crashed and tore off a wing. Lady Bird had to be taken out by car and had a miscarriage because of it.

By the end of the 1950s, the ranch was a place for

their guests to stay, a place to entertain, to have "a good visit" with friends and family, and a place for their own family to escape and rest. Years later Lady Bird wrote of the LBJ Ranch, "For me it means continuity, permanence, and roots."

When Lynda was asked about the ranch and whether they liked it, she replied, "Like it? That's like asking whether a cow likes her calf!" Lynda and Luci both thought of the ranch house as their only real home. They would have been happy living there permanently rather than in an apartment in Austin part of the time and in Washington the rest of the year.

In the early years of their lives, Lynda and Luci did not lack care or love in Texas or Washington. Zephyr Wright, the Johnsons' cook, had been with the family before the girls were born. Helen and Eugene Williams were hired in 1950 to organize the household and to help care for them when Lady Bird was away. Willie Day Taylor became a surrogate mother who lived with the girls in Washington and in Austin.

Lady Bird went to Marshall, Texas, in 1942 to hire Zephyr Wright, a young, black college student, to become their cook. She, a driver, and Zephyr drove from East Texas to Washington. During those years of segregation, whites and blacks had different restaurants and motels. Lady Bird would not stay where she could not find accommodations for her traveling companions. They took turns driving, bought take-out food, and traveled long hours. Zephyr worked for the Johnsons for twenty-seven years and loved Lynda and Luci from birth.

Helen and Eugene Williams answered an ad in an Austin newspaper in 1950 for a couple who would travel. They were hired for a two-week trial and stayed. Helen not only organized the house, she organized the whole family. She packed for Lady Bird and Lyndon and helped care for Lynda and Luci while they were away. Eugene drove for the family and also helped with the girls.

There were some problems of having blacks as members of a white household. Eugene drove Lynda and Luci to different activities and stayed with them if their mother was not present. Once he took the two young girls to a movie in Washington. He was not permitted to go into the theater with them because he was black. When they arrived back home with Lynda still crying because they could not see the movie, their father asked for an explanation. Eugene explained that as a black he was not permitted entrance.

He was also the one to ask that they not have Luci's beagle in their car when they drove from Washington to Austin. He said, "It is hard enough finding a place where we can sleep without having to find someplace that will take a dog, too." They did not have to take the dog.

Willie Day Taylor first met the Johnsons in 1948, when she was a student at The University of Texas at Austin. She had not worked for a month and was deeply in debt. She was trying to work her way through the university and was offered a part-time job in Johnson's Senate race. Her working hours were supposed to be for four hours in the mornings but ended up from early morning until midnight. She worked off and on in Lyndon's Austin office through 1949. Just before Christmas, Taylor went to Washington to work in the office there.

She knew no one in Washington, so the Johnsons invited her to stay with them over Christmas. She fell in love with Luci on first sight. Lynda accepted her but thought Willie Day belonged more to Luci than to her. Willie Day lived with the Johnsons and rode back and forth to work with Lyndon. She eventually moved to her own apartment, where the girls visited for weekends occasionally. Once when the girls were visiting their father in his office, Luci said, "Wi-Day, my Mommy says you can't go places unless you're 'vited." She paused for a moment and then said, "But if you were to 'vite me, I could spend a weekend with you." Willie Day invited her and a pattern began.

In the fall of 1954, she moved into an apartment in

Austin with the girls so they could go to school. They went home to the ranch at Johnson City on the weekends when their parents were there. Then in January she moved to Washington, where the girls lived with their parents and attended school the second semester. Lynda and Luci attended dual schools from 1954 until 1957, in Austin in the fall and Washington in the spring. The Johnsons were told the girls could either go to school in Austin all year or in Washington all year but they couldn't do both. Willie Day moved into the Johnsons' Washington home in the fall of 1957 to care for the girls while Lady Bird and Lyndon were in Austin. They attended school in Washington until they graduated from high school.

Lynda was not close to Willie Day until she became ill when she was ten. She had something similar to rheumatic fever, where the muscles and nerves quiver. She could not attend school for about three months and wanted Willie Day, Helen Williams, or her mother with her at all times because she was scared.

Lynda was enrolled at St. Stephen's, a private school, because they would let her attend one-half day until she became strong enough to attend all day. She was enrolled at St. Stephen's until she went to O. Henry Junior High. Luci went to Mrs. Huberich's School her first two years and then transferred to Casis Elementary.

Even as youngsters Lynda took things more seriously than Luci did. Luci assumed everything would be all right. Lynda was conscientious about schoolwork. If she found an error she had made, she rewrote until everything was correct. Luci just scratched through and wrote corrections above it. Lynda was a perfectionist; Luci wasn't. There was normal rivalry between the sisters, but they grew closer as they matured.

Luci had an eye problem which created reading problems. Willie Day thought she just wanted to be read to but noticed that she remembered things when she was read to that she didn't understand when she read.

Whether it was the eye problem or differences in personalities, Luci was never the scholar that Lynda was.

Christmas was always a favorite time for Lynda and Luci because it meant they were in Texas and with their family. Rebekah Johnson, their only living grandmother, liked having her children and grandchildren with her on Christmas Eve. The tradition was always the same, with colorfully wrapped gifts covering the floor around the tall Christmas tree and the smell of homemade fruitcake. Each year the celebration was the same.

Luci loved animals and begged for a dog. Lyndon bought her first dog, a beagle, when she was three. They named it Little Beagle Johnson so its initials would be the same as the rest of the family's. Luci, who was more outspoken than Lynda, was later to grumble, "In this family, I come just before the dogs!"

Neither of the girls inherited their mother's shyness. Lynda was quiet and dignified and kept her troubles to herself. Luci was more emotional and outspoken. Both were warm and friendly. Lady Bird taught them the value of self-confidence and independence.

Throughout their lives, Lady Bird treated them as adults. Each daughter had her own bank account and allowance before she entered her teen years. Their mother taught them to buy their own clothes within a budget and make their own selections within the framework of her guidelines.

The girls respected their mother and did not want to displease her. She trusted them and they knew it. She never resorted to spanking them, but a disapproving look quickly brought results. Their mother taught them public service and responsibility both by what she said and what she did herself.

Each time Lady Bird became confident that she had their lives organized, something happened to disrupt everything. On Luci's eighth birthday on July, 2, 1955, Lyndon, a heavy smoker, had a severe heart attack. Lady Bird was in Washington preparing for Luci's birthday party when she received the news that Lyndon was being taken by ambulance to Bethesda Naval Hospital. She left immediately and was there when he arrived.

"Stay with me, Bird," he begged. "I'd rather fight with you beside me. I'm sure we'll lick this." He immediately went into shock.

Lady Bird stayed in the hospital with him for six weeks, occupying the room next to his. Lyndon was the Senate leader, and he was determined to inform his colleagues of the seriousness of his attack. He said, "Don't kid anybody. Don't say I'm in for a checkup. Say I had a heart attack — a belly buster."

He wanted Lady Bird with him twenty-four hours a day, laughing and wearing lipstick. And he accepted the realism of death. He had just ordered two suits to be made by his tailor. Since he had lost so much weight in the hospital, Lady Bird asked what he wanted to do about the suits. He said, "We might as well keep the dark blue one, Bird. We'll need that one, either way." Lady Bird laughed.

She was always there when he muttered his first words upon awakening, "Where's Bird?" Outwardly, she remained calm and strong for Lyndon. But to a friend she whispered, "When Lyndon is out of danger and the crisis is past, I just want to go off alone somewhere and cry."

He was in the hospital for six weeks before he was allowed to return to the ranch to recuperate from the attack. For six months the family lived there and became closer than ever. Lady Bird said, "During those days, we rediscovered the meaning and freshness of life." Lynda and Luci played dominoes with their father and read to him. He had time to listen to their daily chatter about what they were doing and about their friends.

Lady Bird struggled with the difficulties he had in quitting the smoking habit and learning new eating habits. She organized their food to fit his diet. She worked with Zephyr on preparing low-calorie foods and measuring everything on new scales. Lyndon had quit smoking three packages of cigarettes a day, but he kept a package on the table by the bed to test his willpower. With Lady Bird's supervision of his food and exercise, he lost from 225 pounds to 180 pounds. By the time they returned to Washington, the family was closer than ever before. Lyndon said, "That heart attack taught me to appreciate some things a busy man sometimes almost forgets. I'm learning all over again how to live."

The heart attack did not change the basic drive of the man. He resumed his Senate duties by early 1956. When reporters asked Lady Bird how she would feel about being First Lady, she replied, "I no more expect it to happen than I do to walk out that door and have lightning strike me."

She may not have foreseen the future in the White House, but she knew that she would always be the wife of a politician. She seemed destined to campaign for her husband for one office or another. To prepare herself for that role, she enrolled in a speech class sponsored by the Capital Speakers' Club with Hester Beall Provensen as her teacher in 1959. At the age of forty-seven, she went back to school to learn speech organization, delivery and platform poise.

Shyness was one of the things that made Lady Bird tense when she stood up to address an audience. She worked hard to overcome that under the supervision and teaching of Mrs. Provensen. Her nervousness made her talk faster, which made her voice pitch higher. Luci often told Lady Bird that her voice was too loud and shrill when she spoke and that she should keep it soft. Lady Bird said, "She was right. When I am under strain I tend to talk loud." Her teacher taught her "reaction time," a time for the words to form into complete thoughts before beginning another sentence or thought.

The class's first assignment was for one classmate to introduce another in a thirty-second statement. The second assignment was to team with another classmate for a presentation and acceptance speech. Her partner for that assignment was the wife of an official at the Australian embassy.

They created a situation: Lady Bird was traveling through Australia on a plane and a friend was meeting her at one stop of the trip to present her a gift. Before they left class the day the assignment was given, Lady Bird asked her partner to telephone and let her know what the imaginary gift was to be so that she could prepare an acceptance speech accordingly. Lady Bird was out of town when her partner telephoned. Her housekeeper answered the telephone, and the crisp-speaking Australian left the message that she was going to present Lady Bird a pair of koalas. The housekeeper, not knowing the circumstances, quickly said, "I don't know what she'll do with them. I look after the children and the dogs, but I can't take care of two koala bears!"

Lady Bird was a good student and learned many things other than voice control. She learned platform procedure, the best kind of clothes to wear so as not to distract from her face when she spoke, how to sit on a platform, and how to stand to look relaxed and most appealing. She became an example for future students to follow. Mrs. Provensen clipped pictures of Lady Bird from the newspapers to use as illustrations for her students to show how to present oneself in speaking. Of the course itself, Lady Bird said, "[I]t turned out to be one of the most delightful, expanding experiences I've ever had."

Her first public speaking at a press conference turned into a family affair, even though she said she was not ready to speak in front of Lyndon. He was supposed to attend a National Press Club dinner, but he slipped away during the entertainment part of the dinner. Lady Bird had just begun answering questions when he arrived. Then Luci and Little Beagle Johnson arrived. Her solo affair became a family affair and went very well.

As the wife of the Senate majority leader, Lady Bird was thrown into the public spotlight more and more because of the speculations about Lyndon running for president in the 1960 election. The rumors had not been denied nor confirmed. His chances of becoming the Democratic candidate were not good. Many of the party considered his Southern birth a detriment to his chances. He was not popular in the South because of his record on civil rights. He guided the Senate through its first civil rights bill since Reconstruction days. He took part in defeating a Southern filibusterer who was trying to stop the bill.

Lyndon did not announce his presidential candidacy until a week before the Democratic Convention, which was to be held in Los Angeles. Lady Bird was not with him on July 5, 1960, when he made the announcement. She was in Marshall, Texas, at the bedside of her father. A television set was brought into his hospital room so she could see and hear her husband. She said, "It was a considerable pulling of the heartstrings to have to hear it from a distance but if I had not come here, and there had been no other chance for me to talk with my father, I would never have forgiven myself."

Lady Bird went to Los Angeles for Speaker Sam Rayburn's nomination of Lyndon for the presidency and was again ready to campaign. She said, "I find it interesting and exhilarating . . . I have learned a lot. I feel it's important for me to go along. I think people can assess a man better when they know what kind of wife and family he has. They are interested in the total man. I can be helpful to him on trips, too . . . I try to remind him of his diet without being obnoxious . . . He's kind enough or flattering enough to value my judgment."

The months of planning diets and caring for Lyndon were paying off. His recent cardiogram showed no evidence of damage from his 1955 heart attack. The four Johnsons set out for Los Angeles and the Democratic Convention. They were met by a group of supporters at the Los Angeles Biltmore Hotel. Each of the Johnsons, beginning with Lyndon, made a comment to the group. Lady Bird and Lynda followed. Thirteen-year-old Luci stole the show when she said, "Gosh, I wish I had as many boy friends as there are people in this room."

The suspense was hard on the family and particularly showed in Lynda Bird and Luci's reaction to the announcement that John F. Kennedy had won the nomination. When it was announced that Kennedy had 761 votes to Johnson's 409, Luci burst into tears.

Lady Bird took the girls to the Biltmore, where they found newsmen waiting for them. To the questions that were fired at her about how she felt, she replied, "I wouldn't be saying what is true if I didn't say that I'm disappointed for my country. Lyndon would have made a noble President . . . a tough, can-do President. But as a mother and a wife and a woman who wakes up in the morning wanting to call her day her own, I have a sizable feeling of relief." Her calm, honest response endeared her to the press, and that endearment has never diminished.

Lady Bird's "feeling of relief" did not last for long. Lyndon Baines Johnson was soon back in the spotlight, which enclosed her in its beam of light. She was rapidly entering a new phase of frantic activity that called on all of her resources to cast off finally the shy, insecure person she had been.

CHAPTER 8

The Campaign Trail

In the spring of 1960, Lady Bird introduced her husband as "an exciting man to live with; an exhausting man to keep up with; a man who has worn well in the twenty-five years we have been together." Her hands still shook with nervousness, but the sparkle in her eyes told of her sincerity. Continued practice and determination to overcome her nervousness enabled her to become the number-one campaigner when Lyndon accepted the number-two position on the Democratic ballot for the 1960 presidential election.

Lady Bird answered the early morning telephone call on Thursday, July 14, 1960, when John F. Kennedy asked for a meeting with Lyndon. "I know he is going to offer you the Vice Presidency, and I hope you won't take it," she told Lyndon. They had been disappointed that the young man from Boston had won the Democratic nomination for the presidency. Lyndon was distressed that he had lost. Lady Bird was sorry, too, but she was relieved that they would not have to sacrifice more of their lives to politics than they already had.

Lady Bird was still with Lyndon when Philip Graham, publisher of the *Washington Post,* arrived before Lyndon's meeting with Kennedy. She started to leave the room but both Graham and Lyndon stopped her, saying that she was needed in making the decision. She advised her husband to see no one but John Kennedy, the nominee. She was still with Lyndon when he made a statement to the press, and they both looked "as though they had just survived an airplane crash." She later said, "It was not a spot he would have sought; he had just not thought about it, but the way it was put to him — that the Party needed him — struck a responsive chord."

Lady Bird emerged as a major force in the Democratic campaign in 1960. She was the most visible woman that the Democrats put before the voters. Jacqueline Kennedy was pregnant and could not carry on an active campaign on her husband's behalf.

Lady Bird set a new record for feminine campaigning in the 1960 election. She traveled 35,000 miles in seventy-one days. She made sixteen appearances by herself in eleven states and attended sixteen receptions with John F. Kennedy's sisters. She made 150 appearances with her husband and gave sixty-five "greeting" talks from the back platform of a campaign train. She refused to call her "greetings" speeches. She held more press conferences in two months than most U.S. presidents hold in a year.

No one would have believed that the campaigning Lady Bird Johnson had been so shy that she had prayed for chicken pox if she had to make a valedictorian address at her high school graduation. Her timidity disappeared on the campaign trail. "The way you overcome shyness," she explained, "is to become so wrapped up in something that you forget to be afraid. Lyndon expects a lot of me, so I have learned not to be afraid anymore."

Her first press conference, on August 23, 1960, was held in familiar surroundings at the Woman's National Democratic Club in Washington. Her first trip was to her

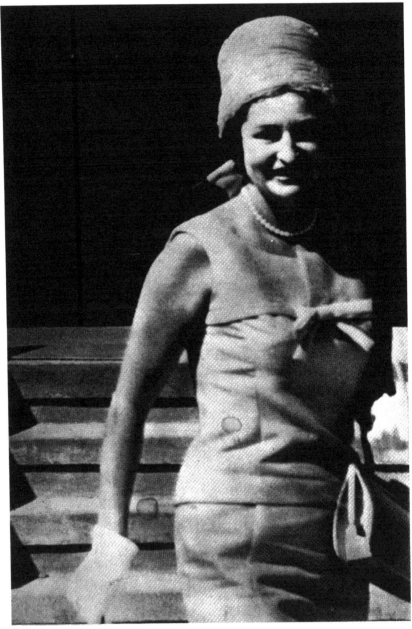

Mrs. Johnson wears a hat for Mr. Potofsky.
— Courtesy LBJ Library

home state. Lady Bird toured Texas in late August with Eunice Shriver, John F. Kennedy's sister, and Ethel Kennedy, Robert Kennedy's wife and the nominee's sister-in-law. She went across Texas four times during the campaign, sometimes with Lyndon and sometimes without. She was a popular campaigner with the men as well as the women.

The high point in her campaigning was a whistle-stop train trip through Alabama. Some twenty-five cousins showed up at the station on one stop to wish her well. There were kinfolks in other states too, and she kept a "kinfolks" file to keep up with them all. A supporter in Alabama gave her a rabbit's foot for good luck, and she carried it with her the rest of the time during the campaign.

As she spoke in Atlanta, a sign above her proclaimed: "Mrs. LBJ is here today, Mr. LBJ is on his way." High overhead, a plane flew back and forth with the words "We love Lady Bird" on a streamer. She looked at the sign and then at the banner and turned to the audience. With a catch in her voice she said, "Nothing like this has ever happened to me before. I can tell you I am powerful proud."

Lyndon sometimes joined her on the spur-of-the-moment without warning. One of those times was in New Orleans, where the city paid the Johnsons the highest honor possible by staging a Mardi Gras motorcade parade out of season.

Lyndon had not planned to remain in New Orleans overnight; therefore, no hotel accommodations had been reserved. Two big conventions were going on, and the hotel was fully booked. The local Democratic leaders persuaded hotel officials to clear a block of rooms for Mr. Johnson and his party. After all arrangements had been made, Lyndon decided not to stay but to go on as originally planned. The leaders who had completed the almost impossible arrangement, not knowing that Lady Bird was in the room, grumbled, "Why can't he make up his mind?" Lady Bird looked up and shouted a firm "Amen!" Everyone laughed and there were no more hard feelings.

She used her sense of humor to relieve many tense situations. She had refused to give in to her fear of flying and used air transportation to appear at as many places as possible. On one trip her airplane skidded off the landing strip in a heavy fog. When the plane finally stopped, she remarked to the frightened women aboard, "Well, chums, it's over!"

Along with her sense of humor, she brought something personal into each speech she made during the campaign. In Oakland County, Michigan, she said, "When I was invited here someone warned me, 'with your southern accent, you'd better take along a translator.' But I'm quite sure that Democrats talk the same language no matter where they are."

In Alexandria, Virginia, she told them that Virginia was very high in her affection because she had many fond memories of taking her mother-in-law over the countryside in search of ancestors and antiques. She was warm and sincere, and that carried through to her audiences.

When a question was raised about opposition in Texas to the issue of Kennedy's Catholicism, Lady Bird replied: "There is such a thing as a religious issue. That we all know. But the more deeply one reads the Bible, the more fair one is going to be. And so, I do not believe it will be a decisive issue in our state."

She was quick to answer questions about medical care for the elderly. Her own father's private finances had enabled him to afford the nursing care that an eighty-six-year-old man required, but people without that advantage would face "financial ruin" when illness came. She was quick to support her stand on medical insurance through government programs that protected the elderly from financial ruin and offered care during their last years.

When a reporter at a press conference asked about Mrs. Kennedy's hairstyle, a teased, bouffant hairdo,

Lady Bird was quick to reply, "I think it's more important what's inside the head than what's outside."

She never evaded questions during her 35,000 miles of travel through the South. "Campaigning might be tiring, if it weren't so much fun," she told an audience in Charlotte, North Carolina. But not all of it was fun.

Less than a week before the election, the Johnsons were campaigning in Texas. They went by motorcade from Fort Worth to Dallas for one of the most memorable days of the campaign. When they arrived in Dallas, they went to the Baker Hotel to change clothes before going to a luncheon at the Adolphus Hotel across the street. A mob was gathered in the street and hotel lobby, but Lady Bird and Lyndon made their way through to the elevator and up to their suite. When they left their hotel to walk across the street to the Adolphus, they became surrounded by the mob. They quickly realized the mob was not a friendly one. They were of the Republican Party and had just seen Richard M. Nixon, their candidate, off at the airport.

People were screaming and waving banners lettered with "traitor," "Yankee," "Civil Rights," and something about "sold out the South." Lady Bird felt "quite steely; that I just had to keep on walking and suppress all emotions and be just like Marie Antoinette in the tumbrel. But I must say that Lyndon was nine times steelier than I was. I think once he was in it, he was determined to make the most of it . . . I was hurt, too, that these were the people we had been working for during the twelve years Lyndon was in the Senate, that we had answered their calls twenty-four hours of the day."

She showed none of those feelings as they moved an inch at a time through the banner-waving group, many wearing Republican buttons. One banner kept hitting her head. She calmly took out her comb and raked it through her hair, which had become messed up during the encounter. She wore a grim smile that did not waver. As they entered the Adolphus, they turned and looked straight at the crowd. For just a few seconds there was absolute silence before someone uttered an ugly comment. Lyndon placed his hands on her shoulders, pushed her toward the ballroom, and whispered, "Don't say anything."

"It was a sad thing," she said later that day. "But I try to look for something constructive in it. I hope every good Democratic friend will be moved because of this to go home and get ten more friends to go out and vote Democratic."

The Lady Bird of 1960 had come a long way from the shy, young woman who dressed in drab clothes to avoid calling attention to herself. On the campaign trail she wore red dresses and suits and ignored her fear of flying to go by chartered plane to reach the rallies.

When she traveled with her husband, she reminded him if he spoke too long or ate too much of the wrong thing or too little of anything. She mended his split trousers in Albuquerque after he rode a horse in a parade. She scolded him when he did not rest and acted as a buffer when she could protect the little time he had to relax.

T. J. Taylor, Lady Bird's father, had been ill for some time. Lady Bird had been with him in July at the beginning of the Democratic Convention. But his health began to deteriorate rapidly in late September. Lady Bird interrupted her campaign schedule to go to Marshall to visit him. When he seemed to become stable, she returned to her own schedule. Three weeks later, he became much worse, and she returned to his bedside. Although she encouraged Lyndon to continue campaigning, he joined her before her father died because "I remember how T. J. accepted me and how much respect I have for him." He died on October 22, 1960. After the funeral they went back to their hectic campaigning schedules.

Lady Bird composed two speeches for the results of the 1960 election. One was for winning and one was for losing. The Johnsons were in Texas on election day and heard the returns in Austin. Lady Bird took her victory speech and revised it to include a message aimed especially for Mrs. Nixon. She added, "And to the other two couples who were our opponents, I would like to extend our best wishes. I am sure they know, as we do, that it is a high privilege to be one of the four couples to appear before one hundred and eighty million American people, asking for the top job."

When the November election was over and John F. Kennedy and Lyndon B. Johnson won, Robert Kennedy said, "Lady Bird carried Texas for us." Her husband did not make a public statement except to give an impulsive kiss to Lady Bird's forehead after he was inaugurated in January 1961.

She set three goals for herself as Second Lady: "helping Lyndon all I can, helping Mrs. Kennedy whenever she needs me, and becoming a more alive me." As wife of the vice-president of the United States, she was exposed to new cultural and public experiences. She accompanied Lyndon in foreign travel and the ceremonial duties that fell to him. Always aware of the environment, she described in detail the beauty of the different countrysides and people. She remarked to a reporter: "As I travel around the world with Lyndon, I often think of that funny old sign on my daddy's store, 'T. J. Taylor, Dealer in Everything.' Now science and time and necessity have propelled the United States to be the general store for the world, dealers in everything. Most of all, merchants for a better way of life, I hope."

During the two years and ten months her husband was vice-president, she traveled more than 120,000 miles with him to thirty-three foreign countries. "My role," she said, "was to be an extra pair of eyes and ears for Lyndon . . . and to give the people of the countries we visited a picture of what women are like in the United States and the role they play in the life of the country."

Lady Bird was a goodwill ambassador who set out to build friendships with people as well as leaders in foreign lands. She was an organized traveler and one with a mission. Carrying a little black notebook everywhere she went, she jotted down notes on her impressions in the shorthand she learned in college. She recorded whom she met and what she saw. She sent word ahead to each country that she was to visit that she wanted to see the "women doers" of the nation. She always had time for reporters at each stop. Many of them were surprised at her humanitarian interests. She was genuinely interested in the welfare of women in all countries.

She often found herself called upon to substitute for the First Lady, Jacqueline Kennedy. One journalist called her "Washington's No. 1 pinch hitter." She greeted women delegates from the United Nations in December 1961 and stood in for her in April 1963 at a luncheon of the Senate Ladies Red Cross group. "I don't know how we could get along without Lady Bird," said one White House aide.

One such occasion was in 1962, when her husband was being honored at a dinner and she was to go with him. At the last minute she received a call from the White House asking her to substitute for Mrs. Kennedy at a dinner where the First Lady was to receive a TV Emmy award for public service. Lady Bird accompanied Lyndon to the first dinner and sneaked out when the dinner began. She took a cab to the second dinner and composed an acceptance address in a phone booth before going to the Emmy award dinner. She accepted the award, made the speech, and returned to the vice-president's dinner. Her husband, famous for "the LBJ trot," could not have done better himself.

Lady Bird's friends, both Democrats and Republicans, had nothing but praise for her. "That's the greatest woman I have ever known," said Speaker of the House Sam Rayburn, who had known her since she and Lyndon were married in 1934. "She's good and she's kind and she never has a mean thought," said Republican Congressman Charles Hallect's wife, Blanche. Democratic Congressmen Hale Boggs's wife, Lindy, once paid a tribute to Lady Bird and then said, "I make her sound like a combination of Elsie Dinsmore and the Little Colonel . . . but this is the problem with Bird. When you talk about her, you make her too good to be true."

Lady Bird knew that some Washingtonians thought she was dull. She said, "They make me feel like putting on red tights and running down Pennsylvania Avenue." Some, like Jackie Kennedy, thought Lyndon ruled her life. Jackie Kennedy said, "If LBJ demanded it, Lady Bird would take off all her clothes and run stark naked down the streets of Washington." Mrs. Kennedy was not charitable toward the woman who filled in for her at Mrs. Kennedy's whim and referred to the Johnsons as "Colonel Cornpone and his little Pork Chop."

Lady Bird never acknowledged negative comments nor gossip and had nothing but positive things to say about anyone who criticized her or Lyndon. Unlike her husband, who read everything written about him, she seldom read anything that mentioned her name. She refused to be drawn into the petty discussion of who spent the most on clothes or what designer was used. "I guess I'm pretty unremarkable as far as clothing goes. No Paris, alas," she said with a smile. In a more serious tone she said, "I like clothes. I like them pretty. But I want them to serve me, not for me to serve them — to have an important but not consuming part of my life."

She busied herself with more important matters. After the election the Johnsons realized they needed a larger house because they would entertain larger groups and more prominent political figures than ever before. Lady Bird again looked for the model house and found it.

Perle Mesta, former United States minister to Luxembourg, a friend of the Johnsons and a top Washington party-giver, had a beautiful French chateau, "Les Ormes," on a hilltop in the Spring Valley section of Washington. She sold the elegant house to the vice-president and his wife. The house had everything: parquet floors in the library, a dining room and a drawing room which had been shipped from France, wood paneling from Versailles, and Waterford crystal chandeliers. The Johnsons changed the name of the house to "The Elms" (Les Ormes in English) and remodeled the kitchen. An office was added for Lady Bird to deal with her personal correspondence, which had increased by 100 percent.

Over the years in Washington, Lady Bird's pattern of entertaining expanded in proportion to her position and surroundings, but the flavor was always the same. She learned something personal about each guest so she could converse with that person on a personal level. She wanted each person to feel as important as anyone else in the room.

When they moved to The Elms in 1961, entertaining took on even larger proportions and was more formal than in her former home. She also gave a series of ladies' luncheons and introduced the practice of having speeches at social luncheons. She asked two or three Senate wives to stand and tell everyone something about their home states. The comments added flavor and enjoyment to the luncheons. The focus on two or three wives at a time also allowed the ladies to get better acquainted with each other and learn something about various states in the country.

She gave luncheons for what she called "women doers" or lady "activists." The guest book the Johnsons kept at The Elms was filled with the hundreds of names of visitors from all over the country who enjoyed their hospitality. She also served as hostess outside her home. The First Lady, Mrs. Kennedy, frequently requested that Lady Bird serve as hostess in her absence. Her philosophy for a successful party was a simple one: "Enjoy the people and let them enjoy themselves."

To keep up with her varied daily schedule she made lists and scratched off items as she moved from a visit to a Peace Corps center in Oklahoma, a ground-breaking ceremony for a public works facility in West Virginia, or the Spanish lessons that she was taking during that time.

She worked on her third goal of "being a more alive me." She was finding her own voice and role in Washington. She saw to it that women in the labor movement who were visiting the city for a strategy conference in January 1962 had an entertaining tea at The Elms, including a talk from the vice-president. In one of her speeches she argued: "American women are undergoing a great revolution in our lifetime. We have learned to master dishwashers, typewriters and voting machines with reasonable aplomb. We must now try to make our laws catch up with what has happened to us as we bounce in and out of the labor market and raise a family."

Lady Bird took her duties as wife of the vice-president very seriously. Shortly after she became Second Lady, she was seated at a dinner next to a Mr. Potofsky. He said, "You have no idea how much you ladies in the news influence fashion and affect our economy." He pointed out that women no longer wore hats because none of the Kennedy women wore them. They had gone out of fashion because of the popular Jackie Kennedy hairstyle. The trend had a telling effect on jobs among the milliners. Lady Bird never forgot Mr. Potofsky and about every third event, she would say, "I'll wear a hat today for Mr. Potofsky."

Lady Bird was just as sensitive to her daughters as she was to her husband's position. Lynda and Luci attended the National Cathedral School in Washington. Willie Day Taylor supervised them when their parents were absent. When Lady Bird was questioned about raising teenagers, she said, "My own recipe for raising them [Lynda and Luci] is to give them a considerable sense of independence and to let them know I trust them a lot, but that I am there to see what comes through."

Lynda and Luci did not want to embarrass or disappoint their parents. About their mother, Lynda said, "We have a moral togetherness. Luci and I always know that whether Mother is with us or not she is thinking of us.

Mother has never told us when to be in from a party or date. She just leaves it to our own good judgement. How can you break faith with a woman who does that?"

If faith was broken, as it was in the case of Luci when she was fourteen, Lady Bird dealt with it swiftly. Luci's date kept her out until one o'clock in the morning. When they arrived home, they were confronted by Lady Bird. The date said, "She chewed us up one side and down the other. Nobody ever made me feel so small."

Lady Bird shared her duties as wife of the vice-president with Lynda and Luci. Luci cut ribbons to open bazaars or flower shows. She took Christmas baskets to the bedside of children too sick to attend the general Christmas party. Lynda traveled abroad with her parents as a teenage goodwill ambassador to Turkey. She was very popular with the Turks. Each time her father stopped the car in the motorcade to speak to the friendly crowds along the route, Lynda stepped out and made short friendship talks to the cheering people.

Jacqueline Kennedy invited Lynda and Luci to a state dinner for the president of Sudan. They thought it was a mistake and quickly wrote her a note to verify their invitation. She assured them that she wanted them to come. They immediately called Lady Bird in Austin to ask how they were supposed to act in the White House. She told them, "Read all you can find in the encyclopedia about the Sudan, and don't drink any of the wine at dinner."

Both girls preferred living in Texas and took every opportunity to be in the state. For many years they both went to Camp Mystic at Hunt, Texas, in the summer. "It was almost like belonging to a lodge or sorority," Lady Bird said, "because I have stood in receiving lines all over the country and had mothers tell me their daughters knew my daughters at Camp Mystic."

Lynda Bird worked as an apprentice at her mother's television station, KTBC, in Austin during the summer between her junior and senior years in high school. She learned everything she could from accounting to switchboard operating. She deposited her dollar-an-hour salary in her own bank account and kept a careful record of everything she earned and spent.

When a friend asked her if she missed Washington and was ready to return to the social whirl, she quickly replied, "No! I want to stay here. Under the new minimum wage law I will make a dollar and fifteen cents an hour after September 1."

In September she did not receive the raise because she had to return to Washington to finish her senior year in high school. When her father heard the story he said proudly, "She has a head for business just like her mother."

Lynda Bird met Bernard (Bernie) Rosenbach on a blind date during the summer she worked at KTBC. He was a tall, blond young man from Comfort, Texas. During her senior year in high school in Washington, she frequently visited him at the Naval Academy where he was a midshipman.

By the time she graduated from high school in 1962, she was wearing his midshipman's pin. At the end of her freshman year at The University of Texas at Austin, she was officially engaged. Her parents gave an engagement party for her at The Elms in June 1963.

That year was a monumental one for the LBJ family. Lynda was engaged to be married. Luci had her sixteenth birthday and received a white Convair convertible. Lady Bird and Lyndon were the most visible Second Family to occupy the position in a long time. Their lives were full and exciting. In the fall, President John F. Kennedy and his wife Jacqueline were scheduled to visit the LBJ Ranch. President Kennedy had been there, but Jackie had been unable to go with him. On the morning of November 22, 1963, Lady Bird had placed fresh fruit in all of the guest rooms and left Zephyr Wright and her kitchen staff making pies for the barbecue dinner that night. She and Lyndon flew to Dallas to meet the president and his wife and accompany them in a motorcade through Dallas.

The morning which began with a fine drizzle turned into a beautiful fall day, pleasantly warm under a clear, blue sky. The crowds were particularly friendly and everyone in the motorcade was in high spirits. There was nothing to remind Lady Bird of the awful day in Dallas when a mob yelled and spat at them in front of the Adolphus Hotel. She was happy to be in her own home state as she held a bouquet of yellow roses, the flower that had almost become her trademark in her travels.

She rode between her husband and Senator Ralph W. Yarborough of Texas, with one Secret Service car between them and the president. They returned greetings and exchanged waves and smiles with the sea of people lining the streets.

President and Mrs. Kennedy were in the lead car of the motorcade with Texas Governor John B. Connally and his wife, Nellie. The special presidential limousine was equipped with a protective glass bubble, but President Kennedy had had the bubble removed so he and his wife could see and be seen more easily.

The momentum of the crowd had built to a high peak of excitement by the time the motorcade reached the eighth mile in its ten-mile trip to the Dallas Trade Mart, where the president was to speak at a luncheon. It was 12:26 P.M. Suddenly, over the applause and cheers of the crowds lining the street, one shot rang out and then two in rapid succession. The motorcade was flanked by motorcycle escorts from the front, along the sides, and at the rear. For a fleeting moment, Lady Bird thought the sound was the backfire from a motorcycle. When the next two shots came in rapid succession, she thought it was firecrackers.

The occupants of the lead car seemed to disappear before her eyes. "Let's get out of here!" someone yelled over the intercom car radio. Secret Service agent Rufus Youngblood jumped over the front seat of the car and threw himself over Lyndon, pushing him to the floor. "Get down!" he yelled at Lady Bird and Senator Yarborough.

When their car stopped in front of Parkland Hospital, Lady Bird was gripped with a terrible foreboding of tragedy. She was in a state of shock as she watched President Kennedy and Governor Connally being carried on stretchers into the hospital. Jacqueline Kennedy walked at her husband's side and Nellie Connally followed her husband's stretcher. Lyndon was immediately taken into a room under the protection of Secret Service.

Lady Bird, Senator Yarborough, and Texas Congressman Jack Brooks found Jacqueline Kennedy standing dazed outside an emergency room in which doctors were frantically working over her husband. Jackie already knew the truth. Her husband was dead. She had held his blood-splattered body against her on that nightmarish ride to the hospital. Lady Bird, not knowing that the president was dead, went to her, put her arms around her, and said, "God help us all."

She went to find Nellie Connally, her friend of almost thirty years. The two women hugged each other and cried. John Connally was in critical condition from a gunshot wound. They did not know at that time if he would survive.

After Lady Bird had comforted both Jackie Kennedy and Nellie Connally, she went to the hospital room where Lyndon was being kept. He was with the president's top aide, Kenny O'Donnell, and White House Associated Press Secretary Malcom Kilduff. O'Donnell, whose face told the message before the words were spoken, said, "The president is dead." Kilduff addressed Lyndon as "Mr. President," and Lady Bird knew the reality of the nightmare. John Kennedy *was* dead. Lyndon's order, "Tell the children to get a Secret Service man with them," struck terror in her heart.

Unmarked cars were brought to the hospital to take the group to Love Field Airport, where *Air Force One,* the president's airplane, was waiting. Lady Bird later wrote, "Our departure from the hospital and approach to the cars was one of the swiftest walks I have ever made." At that time, no one knew who had fired the shots or how many people were involved.

President Johnson had all sirens stopped, and they were driven in separate cars to the airport. The cars were traveling as fast as they could safely go. Lady Bird looked at the passing scenery and saw a flag flying at half-mast atop a building. "I think that was when the enormity of what happened first struck me," she said.

Judge Sarah Hughes arrived at 2:25 P.M. to administer the presidential oath to the vice-president. By that time Jacqueline Kennedy had arrived at the airfield with her husband's body in a casket. With Lady Bird standing on his right side and Jackie Kennedy on his left side, Lyndon Baines Johnson officially became the thirty-sixth president of the United States. His first act as president was to turn to Lady Bird and kiss her on the forehead.

Suddenly, the three years Lady Bird had spent as Second Lady proved to be training time for her immediate step to First Lady.

CHAPTER 9

The First Lady

The shock of President Kennedy's death and Lyndon's becoming president did not have time to wear off before Lady Bird had to begin making decisions to fill her role as First Lady. "I feel as if I am suddenly on stage for a part I never rehearsed," the new First Lady confessed to Nellie Connally several days after the tragedy.

She assured President Kennedy's widow that she should take as much time as was needed for her to leave the White House. She made arrangements to sell The Elms, her beloved home in Washington, and to distance herself even further from her business interests.

When she was questioned about when the First Family would move into the White House, she replied, "I wish to heaven I could serve Mrs. Kennedy's happiness . . . I can at least serve her convenience . . . It is only when the last chore she wishes to do is done that I will contemplate moving." The Johnsons invited Jacqueline to keep the nursery school she had established there for her children and their playmates.

Lady Bird tried to help her daughters in the transi-

Lady Bird addressing the White House Conference on Natural Beauty, May 1965.

— Courtesy LBJ Library

tion from having reasonably private lives to becoming objects of the press. Sixteen-year-old Luci was living at home and attending National Cathedral School in Washington. Nineteen-year-old Lynda was a student at The University of Texas at Austin. From the day of President Kennedy's assassination, they were joined by Secret Service agents and hounded by the press.

In the midst of all the changes in their lives, Lady Bird had to deal with over 200,000 letters and telegrams that arrived. People had sent condolences on the death of the president and well-wishes for the enormous task the Johnsons had inherited as First Family. She had always responded to her mail. It worried her that she could not possibly answer all of them herself, but, she said, "My friends will think it mighty strange if I don't."

The problem was solved by friends and congressmen's wives, who went to The Elms and worked in relays until all of the mail was answered. It was an act that showed love and respect for Lady Bird, not because she was First Lady but because she was their friend.

The public recognized Lady Bird as an individual separate from her husband. *The Washington Post* called her "a lady of exceptional grace" who had given "unstinting and indefatigable public service" as Second Lady. She told a reporter: "I'd be a vegetable if I didn't have an omnivorous curiosity about the wide, wide, world and Lyndon's position has given me an unparalleled opportunity to be exposed to it both at home and abroad."

The Johnsons had been visible as the vice-president's family representing the Kennedy administration. Lady Bird had traveled over 120,000 miles to dozens of countries with Lyndon. They had made contact with heads of state in foreign countries, in their Washington home, and at the LBJ Ranch in Texas.

She used the knowledge and experience as Second Lady to become the most active First Lady since Eleanor Roosevelt. When she moved into the White House early in December, the first thing she did was to acquaint herself with the 132-room mansion. "My first job," she decided, was "to make this home a place where Lyndon can operate productively, and to add to his operation in every way that I can, because I never felt so much need on his part, and so much compassion on my part for him."

She supervised the $680,000-a-year household budget for the White House as she had done her own business — with thrift and budgetary rules. Although she told Chief Usher J. B. West that she wanted him to run the White House, she soon was doing it herself "rather like the chairman of the board of a large corporation." J. B. West was instructed: "Anything that's done here, or needs to be done, remember this: my husband comes first, the girls second, and I will be satisfied with what's left."

One of the first things she did just for herself was to establish a combination office and dressing room in the southwest corner of the second floor of the White House. She put her own furniture in it: a blue velvet sofa, two comfortable French armchairs, and a desk that she had used in each of her homes. It was in this room that she recorded her life in the White House often between the hours of 7:00 in the evening until 9:00 or 10:00 with a sign on the door, "a tiny pillow about the size of an eyeglass case," that simply stated, "I want to be alone." She recorded nearly 1,750,000 words, and one-seventh of the typed manuscript became *A White House Diary,* which was published in 1970. She was the first First Lady to leave such a legacy of historical record of life as the wife of the president of the United States.

Although Lady Bird enjoyed good press coverage from her earliest days in the White House, she asked Elizabeth Carpenter, a Washington journalist and friend, to become her staff director and press secretary. Bess Abell continued as her social secretary. Liz Carpenter said of Lady Bird, "She knew the language of the trade, the difference between an AM and PM deadline, that it is better to be accessible than evasive . . . She treated reporters with warmth and respect."

Lady Bird's background in journalism, television, and politics gave her an understanding of the working press. She also knew that the women reporters who had been assigned to cover her could determine the success of any programs that she wanted to do as First Lady. She said, "It was a whole new adjustment for me — having every move watched and covered and considered news." She began to have teas "to set the tenor of press conferences — not as conferences but informal meetings — an invitation to a relaxed and pleasant atmosphere with an opportunity to meet somebody else who was newsworthy." The teas grew into "women doer" luncheons, where the guests heard women who were active in different positions and could answer public questions. Press representatives were always invited to the luncheons.

Lady Bird was not an active feminist, but she was concerned about the lack of recognition of women. She felt that the government had paid too little attention to women, their needs, and the contributions they could make to the country. She frequently pointed out these facts to her husband through the years of their marriage. When he became president, he was aware of the potential among "women doers." He said when he came home from the office, Lady Bird always asked, "Well, what did you do for women today?" More women were appointed to government positions by President Johnson than any other period of time before his presidency.

Lady Bird was not an active conservationist in the fall of 1963. She later wrote that she was "an enjoyer, somebody who gets pleasure from the beauty around me. It had not yet occurred to me that I could do anything about making sure that the beauty remained here for our children and our grandchildren or about trying to see that there was even more of the beauty, but that would come."

She saw her role as First Lady to be one that "must

emerge in deeds, not words." The trip to the Pennsylvania coal mines in January 1964 is typical of her many deeds. The president had made his War on Poverty speech, when Lady Bird visited the cities of Wilkes-Barre and Scranton, "the sort of depressed places Lyndon had in mind." It was a day of running from one area to another with little rest in between. She was greeted and given a key to the city and then visited the Wyoming Valley Technical Institute. There coal mine workers were retrained in other skills: woodwork, machinery, auto repair, painting, and paperhanging. She spoke personally to several of the trainees and offered encouragement for their efforts.

In March 1964, Lady Bird and former President Harry S Truman represented the president of the United States at the funeral of King Paul of Greece. Several days after arriving home, Lady Bird wrote in her diary, "I must say that being with President Truman those days has been one of the big pluses of this period of my life. It has been an insight into history for me, a joy to see a man who has lived through so much public rancor and condemnation and has emerged philosophic, salty, completely unembittered, a happy man — and vindicated by history on most of his major decisions."

A major decision made in the life of the Johnsons was that Lyndon would run for reelection in 1964. No First Lady had campaigned for her husband before that time, but Lady Bird took to the campaign trail with as much enthusiasm as she had for the 1960 election. There was resentment in the Southern states over the civil rights legislation that the president was sponsoring. "Don't give me the easy towns, Liz," she told her press secretary, Elizabeth Carpenter. "Anyone can get into Atlanta — it's the new, modern South. Let me take the tough ones."

She did a whistle-stop tour from Washington to New Orleans in three days. She traveled 1,682 miles through eight states and made forty-seven stops. She appealed to

Southerners with her love of the South, her belief in their fairness and their willingness to support the constitutional rights of all Americans. Although she encountered heckling in some places, the tour was a huge success. When she returned to Washington, Lyndon called her "one of the greatest campaigners in America" and said, "I'm proud to be her husband."

The president was not only proud of Lady Bird, but he depended on her as "the last sounding board, the last reasoner, the voice of calm, and remarkable understanding." Jack Valenti, a presidential aide, wrote that the president valued her opinion "because he knew that, alone among his entourage, she delivered her views without any self-interest or leashed ego that may have been hidden in the breasts of all of the rest of us."

She was interested in the Great Society poverty programs and visited areas to check on the progress of communities. "I want to go down to see what the Teachers Corps is doing in Appalachia," Lady Bird said to Liz Carpenter one day. "See what you can work out." Her request produced a three-day trip called "Adventure in Learning."

Prior to any of her trips, an advance person, often Nash Castro, was sent to make all of the arrangements for her visit. He worked out transportation, the route of the motorcade, and released advance publicity to attract a crowd. On her trip to Appalachia, one of the most interesting stops she made was in Canada Township, North Carolina. The town was an hour and a half's drive from Ashville, where she was to visit schools and a mountain family, Mr. and Mrs. Eldon Mathis.

Nash Castro wrote to Lady Bird and advised her to "PLEASE WEAR A PAIR OF EXPENDABLE SHOES" (the road to the house was dirt and likely to be muddy) and "PLEASE WEAR A LOOSE SKIRT" (she would have to jump over a small stream and climb through a low fence to get to the Mathis' yard).

The Mathises had seven children, but as poor as they

were, they kept all seven children in school. Lady Bird discussed crops that the family raised and gave them a jar of peach preserves from the LBJ Ranch. She said, "We asked the Home Demonstration woman to come to the ranch and show us how to preserve this." In her way she never gave advice, but she implied ways to learn. The group visited the Canada Township school, ate lunch off a tray with the students, shook hands with the teachers, and boarded the bus to go to more schools.

On every trip Lady Bird took, a group of reporters was with her. The reporters were assigned to the First Lady, and they or their respective newspapers or periodicals paid for their expenses. Lady Bird did not try to sell the reporters on her husband's programs, but they learned through her eyes about rural poverty and the stumbling steps the government had begun taking to lend a hand.

Lady Bird accepted as many invitations to speak as her schedule allowed. She was often invited to speak at colleges and universities which she enjoyed because of the contact with young people. Before her visit to an institution, an advance person screened everything to avoid any embarrassment to her or the institution where she was visiting. In one report on a screening, the advance man stated that there was a "slightly calculated risk because there will be 15–25 young writers. There are always one or two oddballs among them."

Liz Carpenter wrote in her book *Ruffles and Flourishes*: "We traveled 200,000 miles to plant trees on mountaintops and in ghettos, to open schools in Appalachia, to visit the Head Start projects of a Newark slum, to walk through the fields of bluebonnets in a Texas pasture. From San Simeon perched above the surging Pacific to a mountaineer's shack in North Carolina, from Cape Kennedy to the redwood forests, we traveled by rubber raft, bus, ski lift, surrey, orchard wagon, rail and foot, and in Mrs. Johnson's least favorite vehicle of all, jet plane."

Nothing seemed to prevent Lady Bird from keeping

to her schedule. She flew to Cleveland on April 21, 1964, on a speech-making tour. Lightning twice struck the plane in which she and a group of forty-four secretaries, reporters, pilots, and staff were flying. She refused to fly back to Washington in the plane. They hired cars and the long caravan drove 450 miles in rain and fog, taking breaks to stop for gas and a meal of cheeseburgers and French fried onion rings. The carburator clogged up on Lady Bird's car and had to be repaired before the tired First Lady arrived back in Washington at 1:30 A.M.

The Johnsons were described in the press as generous, fortunate, sophisticated, wholly unspoiled, or folksy individuals by reporters who liked them. One description that was used by all was that the Johnsons were the most hospitable of all First Families. During their five years in the White House, they entertained over 200,000 guests. Most were planned social occasions, but the president was still a spur-of-the-moment host. "Bird, let's have Congress over this afternoon," he said to Lady Bird one morning. Congress came and everything was ready. Chief Usher West described the Johnsons as "the dancingest First Family" he had ever known.

Not all of the press liked the informal atmosphere that the Johnsons created. They were criticized for "downgrading the dignity of the White House" by discarding many white-tie affairs. When Burmese officials were to be entertained at a formal dinner at the White House, they requested that they be able to wear business suits. Formal wear in their country was native costume and their wives would already be in long dresses. Lady Bird felt the press would criticize them, but the president decided to honor the Burmese officials' wishes regardless of the negative response of the press.

The president and Lady Bird were not the only ones hounded by the press. The Associated Press wrote about Lynda and Luci: "If one of the girls dances cheek-to-cheek, it's front page news. If she diets, her weight is a

State Department secret. If she is engaged, ninety million females and some males want to see the ring."

One young man remarked: "It takes guts to date them. You become public property after your first movie and engaged on your second hamburger." Public opinion was not as important to some dates as the opinion of Lynda and Luci's father. One of Luci's dates complained: "He looks at boys like he looks at lobbyists. He just sits there and sizes them up, and a Lyndon Johnson size-up can scare the fool out of you."

Luci was more uninhibited and outspoken than Lynda and was often quoted in the press. Lynda remarked to a friend, "I don't necessarily think I owe my life to the American people." In contrast, Luci's statement was: "We don't get paid, but we sure get criticized."

The thing that upset Luci most was when the Johnson women were criticized for the way they dressed. When *Women's Wear Daily* gave them bad marks as dressers in February 1966, Luci was furious. She blamed it on Lynda for wearing bobby socks and loafers.

The White House years for Lynda and Luci were the years of early adulthood when many decisions were made. They were also the years of sibling rivalry. In 1966, Lady Bird wrote in her diary: "And now in a way, it's daughter against daughter. Luci has certain qualifications that make her wonderful with the press and Lynda has characteristics that give her a bad time with them."

Lynda broke her engagement to Bernie Rosenbach and later dated George Hamilton, the movie star. She graduated from the University of Texas cum laude. On December 9, 1967, she married Charles Robb in a White House wedding. She was the first White House bride since Eleanor Wilson, daughter of President Woodrow Wilson, was married in 1914. The Robbs' first child, a daughter named Lucinda, was born on October 24, 1968.

Luci took instructions in Catholicism and was baptized into the Roman Catholic Church on July 2, 1965.

She attended Georgetown University School of Nursing for one year before marrying Patrick Nugent on August 6, 1966, in the National Shrine of the Immaculate Conception. Their first child, named Patrick Lyndon, was born on June 21, 1967. He was the first grandchild of Lady Bird and the president.

Lady Bird put aside her duties as First Lady to be mother to her daughters as the need arose. She had the unique ability to divide her life into compartments. Whatever she was doing at the moment had her undivided attention, but she often shifted from one thing to another without losing concentration on the problem at hand.

The amount of correspondence she received as First Lady was staggering. Both she and the president had a staff that dealt with nothing but letters, invitations, and gifts. Neither could answer all of the mail individually as they had for many years. Anything addressed to President and Mrs. LBJ went directly to her staff. The president always responded personally with appreciation for kind words about Lady Bird. He wrote to Dorothy Schiff of the *Washington Post*: "I told Lady Bird about your kind words, and she appreciated them so much, and so did I. Next to hearing praise about me, I like best to hear it about her!"

When a request came for the president that he could not do but felt was important, he simply wrote Lady Bird a note: "I wish you would do this." She fulfilled all of his personal requests. When the First Lady's schedule became too hectic, Liz Carpenter informed the president's staff: "SOS — Mrs. Johnson just can't take on any more commitments this summer . . . when someone invites the President, you do *not* suggest her as an alternative."

Many invitations for the First Lady to participate in events had to be refused. The Johnsons were asked to preside over meetings for everything from agriculture fairs to give their blessing by appearing at auctions. There were even invitations for their dogs to accept awards or medallions. Newspapers and cookbook writers asked for Lady Bird's recipes. Publications often sent articles that mentioned the Johnsons for their comment before printing. It was a White House rule that no one comment on any article, so all were returned unread.

Both the president and Lady Bird responded to the hundreds of requests for autographed photos, often with a personal note. The following letter is typical of the letters they received from children.

Cindy Willcox ③

170 Fordham Cr.

Pueblo, Colo.

81005

EXECUTIVE

PP6-1/W*

AUTOGRAPH FILE/W*

PP5/Johnson, Mrs. L. B.

[annotations: rec'/ (#10#, 8×10, sgd "Lyndon B. Johnson", "Lady Bird Johnson", 5×7 photo, face, of Pres's days, returning (blank slips of paper 7/20/65]

Mr. President + Family

White House

Washington, D.C.

proc in B.J.

Dear President Johnson + Family,

My friends have dared me to write you + get your family's autographs. I am collecting autographs, any way. Please do me this one favor. Enclosed are some papers to have you sign. They are in an envelope.

Thank you for your cooperation.

Love,

Cindy

#×2Willcox

1965

With best wishes

and the Master of the Pups,

Him   *Her*

An 8 x 10 photo signed by "Lyndon B. Johnson" and "Lady Bird Johnson," a 5 x 7 photo of the president and his dogs, and the signed slips of paper were sent to the writer, Cindy Wilcox of Pueblo, Colorado, within days of receiving the letter in the White House.

Lady Bird occasionally yearned for anonymity, an opportunity to do something on her own without being recognized. She liked to escape the cameras and reporters. One time she put on sunglasses, a big tweed coat and tied a scarf around her head. With her friend and staff member Elizabeth Rowe she walked from the White House to a triangle in front of the Health Education Welfare (HEW) building where gardeners (Federal Park Service) were planting azaleas. Secret Service agents were watching her, but they were at a distance so that they would not call attention to her.

She knew that the azalea bushes were a gift from the city of Norfolk, Virginia. After they had watched the planting for a while, Lady Bird asked one of the old gardeners, "Are those azaleas from Norfolk?" He put down his shovel, looked at them for a minute and asked, "How did you know? Are you girls from Norfolk?" One of the younger men recognized Lady Bird and they all laughed when she said, "No, we're both from Washington."

Lady Bird had escaped public exposure for a short while, but she also respected her position and the press. She had become involved in the beautification of America project in December 1964. She knew that with her influence as First Lady and good coverage by the press the program had a good chance of succeeding. She put her heart and energy into the project which affected all of America.

CHAPTER 10

The First Lady's Project

Several months before Lady Bird's active participation in a specific project as First Lady, she lay the foundation in her speeches. To the Federated Democratic Women of Ohio she said, "We are — and women particularly are — cleaning up the cities of our country." In another speech she referred to the beauty of the landscape when she said, "We saw the beautiful autumn face of Connecticut — those lovely golds and reds of the trees, the most charming memory one could have."

It wasn't until November 1964 that the Task Force on Natural Beauty reported to the president that Lady Bird made the decision to make the beautification of America her project as First Lady. Secretary of the Interior Stewart Udall said that the report was "the most perceptive and creative of the task force reports we have scrutinized."

Task force member Charles Haar said in a cover letter for the report that there was "a great and growing popular demand for an improvement in the quality of the environment." The report itself stated that "the time was never better for action to conserve the natural beauty of this land." The task force made several recommendations to the federal government: national programs for the preservation of landscape and open spaces; beautified highways and regulated billboards; useful parks and forest lands; and rehabilitated city parks.

Lady Bird saw the task force's report and talked to Stewart Udall about it. He suggested that she make Washington, D.C. the model city for the rest of America. "Washington is a shabby city," Udall told her. The *Washington Post* described it as a city of "many lawns, delapidated sidewalks, ugly and confusing clutter of traffic signs, decrepit benches, forbidding trash baskets, hideous parking lots, poorly lit, deserted, and crime-ridden city parks."

There were two distinct parts of Washington: the "Official Washington" and the "Other Washington." The "Official Washington" was made up of monuments, parks, and public buildings. The "Other Washington" was where most of the city's residents lived. The entire Washington area had major problems with pollution, highway location and construction, public transportation, and a decaying inner city.

Once she had decided on a project, Lady Bird sought many opinions before setting up her beautification committee. She had several personal campaigns under way by the end of 1964 in addition to the plans to beautify Washington, D.C. One of the first things she began was to improve the looks of the nation's highways and to remove junkyards and billboards that cluttered the countryside.

President Johnson placed new emphasis on beauty in his State of the Union message on January 4, 1965. The president told Congress that same evening "for over three centuries the beauty of America has sustained our spirit and enlarged our vision." He emphasized that it was now time to "protect this heritage." He was in favor of more parks, improved landscaping on highways,

*President and Mrs. Johnson at the signing of the Highway
Beautification Act, 1965.*

— Courtesy LBJ Library

streets and open spaces, and the legal authority for the government to block air and water pollution.

When Lady Bird was asked how much input she had in the president's speech, she said, "I have lived with it and helped hammer it out. I can't say I helped write it, but some of my own thoughts and hopes came through." She noted in her diary at that time that she hoped they could accomplish some of the beautification projects during their time in the White House.

Laurance Rockefeller was chosen to coordinate the White House Conference on Natural Beauty. President Johnson delivered a message on natural beauty on February 8 and announced that the conference was to meet in May. He urged the nation to "introduce into all our planning, our programs, our building and our growth, a conscious and active concern for the values of beauty."

On February 11, the First Lady's Committee met in the Blue Room of the White House. She told the committee that their goal should be "to implement what is already underway, supplement what should be underway, and to be the catalyst for action" in the beautification of Washington. The members agreed to plant flowers in the traffic triangles and squares, to give awards for neighborhood beautification, and to endorse existing projects.

Lady Bird's first interview on the program was published in the February 22, 1965, issue of *U.S. News and World Report*. She told reporters: "There is a great interest in beautifying the landscape. It seems to me to represent a basic hunger, or yearning, that has spread throughout the whole country." When asked if there was more to beautification than "beauty for beauty's sake," she answered, "Ugliness is so grim. A little beauty, something that is lovely, I think, can help create harmony which will lessen tensions." She predicted that "public feeling is going to bring about regulation, so that you don't have a solid diet of billboards on all the roads."

She concluded the interview with: "The time is ripe — the time is now — to take advantage of this yeasty, bubbling desire to beautify our cities and our countryside. I hope all Americans will join in this effort." The general popular response was enthusiastic. Lady Bird had to set up a separate office and staff to handle the mail for her new program.

Lady Bird never believed a simple "clean-up campaign" would solve the problem. She was concerned for the overall effect on the environment. She wanted to involve as many citizens as possible in the campaign. She hoped to be inspirational in getting citizens to beautify their own surroundings, thus changing the face of an entire neighborhood or community.

She planted her first azaleas at the triangle between Maryland and Independence avenues, at Third Street, S.W., on March 9, 1965, the second meeting of her committee. By the third meeting in April, Mary Lasker had donated more than 9,000 azaleas for Pennsylvania Avenue. The Japanese government had given the roots for 4,000 cherry trees. Laurance Rockefeller gave $100,000 to be used in part to improve the Watts Branch area, thirty-six acres in a low-income part of northeast Washington. A portion of the donation was to be used in cleaning green oxide from statues in the city.

In May, Lady Bird began a series of tours devoted solely to her beautification campaign. She felt that her presence was needed in areas of the nation that had scenic beauty or where there were environmental problems. She also needed "to escape from behind that big iron fence around the White House once in awhile and get the feel of the country." She liked "to get out in the open and come to terms with things."

Her first trip was to the historic sites in Virginia that made up "Landscapes and Landmarks." That visit set the pattern for future trips. She and the committee members who accompanied her were followed by a press bus with forty press reporters and crews from all the major television networks. Lady Bird did not tell the press about areas and projects; she *showed* them the conditions and the improvements.

The White House Conference on National Beauty began on Sunday, May 23, with closed sessions of the panelists. Lady Bird opened the conference the next day with: "In the catalogue of ills which afflict mankind, ugliness and the decay of our cities and countryside are high on America's agenda." Laurance Rockefeller challenged the group to find "new, practical ideas for solving specific problems" and identified "the city, the countryside, and the highways as the broad topics for scrutiny."

The general impression of the conference was favorable but there were some criticisms. Some of the participants complained that it was not well organized, and others grumbled that not enough was done about highway beautification and outdoor advertising. Many years later Henry Diamond said, "The word went out from the White House that the President and the First Lady cared." For Mr. Diamond the meeting was "a major transition — a bridge from the traditional conservation to the new environmentalism and the start of something grand."

Two groups worked simultaneously on the Washington project. One group partially supported by Mary Lasker's donations was concerned with improvements along Pennsylvania Avenue where tourists visited. Also the buildings in that area were monumental. Walter Washington and Polly Shackleton concentrated on the black population in the inner city. Their area of improvement was in schools, playgrounds, and housing projects.

Lady Bird took many trips around Washington the first few months of 1965. She noted areas that needed improvement and often made suggestions as to what could be done in the least expensive way. She reminded her associates "to remember we are using public funds to carry out these beautification projects" and "to use them wisely and well."

She was always aware that the press was necessary

to the success of the program. She advised Nash Castro to take many "before" and "after" photographs of all park-sites where the committee planted floral plants. On November 25, 1965, the American Broadcasting Company (ABC) aired a one-hour television special: "A Visit to Washington with Mrs. Lyndon B. Johnson on Behalf of a More Beautiful Capital." The program pointed out the contrast between the beauty of the historical monuments and the environmental problems of pollution and decay. Stewart Udall wrote Lady Bird after the program: ". . . maybe your ripple will become a wave."

Private funding was necessary to the success of the program. Mary Lasker organized the Society for a More Beautiful National Capital, which collected $25,000 by midsummer and another $11,000 by the end of the year. In January, 1966 Mary Lasker donated $70,000 in matching funds to plant cherry trees at Haines Point. Through Mary Lasker's and Laurance Rockefeller's efforts, many private donors pledged financial support for the Washington project.

On November 30, 1966, Stewart Udall told the First Lady's Committee: "We can give a cheer or two that 25,000 new trees have been planted in Washington. This is a city of trees. Mrs. Johnson's program is showing the Nation that we do not have to wait for the millennium or the construction of new, clean cut cities, but that here and now, in the 1960's, we can renew the old cities, and have new dimensions of beauty and delight."

Generous donations from private sources were not enough to maintain the improvements. Government money was necessary for the success of the program since the Parks Service provided the upkeep of the projects. By the time the effects of the projects were evident, the country was in a state of conflict over the Vietnam War. Money became an issue in providing services that could be cut and used for essential programs. There was congressional opposition to using government money for beautification, a nonessential program.

Lady Bird did not give up; she was determined to keep the effort moving. Private donations continued to be pledged and 1967 became the "Year of the Shade Tree — Bench — Trash Cans." The shade tree theme continued into 1968. Again through Mary Lasker's efforts, private donations paid for trees to be planted. Some of the private funds were diverted to the Parks Service for continued maintenance. Congresswoman Julia Butler Hansen (D. — Wash.), who had opposed government funds for beautification, acknowledged that Washington had "improved a thousand percent within the eight years I have been here."

The landscape was not the only improvement or addition to Washington. Lady Bird's impact on the monumental features of the city was impressive. Pennsylvania Avenue was completely rehabilitated as part of the city's culture and commerce. She was ultimately responsible for the acquisition of the Joseph Hirshhorn art collection and the creation of the Hirshhorn Museum.

The most obvious of Lady Bird's beautification projects was seen in the passing of a national billboard regulation law. Her personal interest and activities in preserving roadside beauty were instrumental in the passage of the Highway Beautification Act of 1965. The law required that states control outdoor advertising along federally funded interstate and primary highways. Controversy over the control of outdoor advertising was nothing new. Disagreements had gone on at the local and state levels since the beginning of the twentieth century. Popular interest in billboard control surfaced again in the early 1960s.

Lady Bird noticed during her car trips from Texas to Washington that the highways were littered with junkyards and billboards. Those experiences deepened her concern about highway beautification and national environment. In 1964, the president called Luther Hodges (then secretary of commerce) and said: "Lady Bird wants to know what you are doing about all those junkyards along the highways." The Bureau of Public Roads made a hasty check and estimated that there were over 16,000 junkyards along the nation's highways, with 1,602 in Texas, the most in any state.

In his State of the Union message on January 4, 1965, the president said: "A new and substantial effort must be made to landscape highways and to provide places of relaxation and recreation wherever our roads run." He supported Lady Bird throughout the controversy over billboard control and highway beautification and involved her in the decision-making process on the issue. She involved herself by following the progress of the bill through the House and Senate committees, participating in strategy conferences and coordinating lobbying as well as doing some herself.

The billboard, junkyard, and scenic highway proposals of the Johnson administration took on the label of "Lady Bird's bill." She was unique in her involvement as a First Lady in the legislative process. In letters that Lady Bird wrote that fall, she said, "Isn't it wonderful that Congress has made highway beautification the law of the land?"

The immediate reaction to the passage of the law on October 22, 1965, was "Lady Bird wins on billboards." The people in the outdoor advertising business were not so kind. The owner of a Dallas company wrote to the president: "This legislation is just a WHIM of Mrs. Johnson." In Montana a billboard appeared briefly asking for the "Impeachment of Lady Bird." But thousands of billboards were quickly removed from the highway right-of-ways.

For a short period of time after the criticism over the billboard law, Lady Bird became less visible. But she was not less active in her approval and support of beautification of highways. She understood the power of publicity around the First Lady, and she wanted it to have a unifying and nonpartisan effect on the American public. She knew how to get the best coverage from the press.

Her working relationship with the press caused

Americans to look at the beauty of their country. Lady Bird encouraged travel by tumbling down rivers on rubber rafts, climbing mountains, and visiting national parks. She loved America, which was undergoing a facelift, and she wanted everyone to share it. In less than five years, she made forty trips with the press for the beautification projects.

As the face of America grew lovelier, the war in Vietnam became uglier. People became more critical of the president's actions in that involvement. Americans had been in Vietnam since the 1950s, but involvement had grown from 15,000 Americans serving as "advisors" in Southeast Asia to nearly nine million, of whom 47,000 would die.

On March 31, 1968, the president announced that he would not seek reelection. The nation was divided by racial strife and the war in Vietnam. The president did not feel he could unite the different factions. He had wavered back and forth for several months, trying to make the decision.

During his presidency he had initiated legislation dealing with poverty, education, Medicare for the elderly, and civil rights — all dreams of the Great Society. He had pushed for legislation to do away with the poll tax, which kept many blacks from voting. Through his efforts to push legislation for desegregation and equal rights, doors had opened for black men and women to be elected judges, sheriffs, congressmen, city mayors, and state governors. He had asked Congress for 115 laws for his Great Society. Ninety of them passed. "When, one day, there is a black president," a civil-rights leader said, "he can thank Lyndon."

During their five years in the White House, the Johnsons laid the foundation for the environmentalism that followed. Lady Bird had instilled conservation and ecological ideas in the national mind. Her understanding and skill in that area ranked her at the top of the scale among modern First Ladies. She never lost the kinship with the land and its natural beauty that she had felt as a child in the flower fields of East Texas.

Lady Bird ceased being First Lady on January 20, 1969, Inauguration Day for President Richard Nixon. After a long, exhausting day of emotional farewells to friends in Washington, the Johnsons returned to the LBJ Ranch. Her last entry in the diary that she had kept during her years as First Lady was closed with a poem from *India's Love Lyrics*: "I seek, to celebrate my glad release, the Tents of Silence and the Camp of Peace." And then she wrote: "And yet it's not quite the right exit line for me because I have loved almost every day of these five years."

Lady Bird continued her beautification work in the post-White House years in Texas. She held annual awards ceremonies at the LBJ Ranch to honor the highway beautification programs of the Texas Highway Department. She hoped that the recognition of the highway officials would encourage in others "a growing sense of the importance of projects that save and use plant material so that we might realize the ecological benefits as well as enjoy the aesthetic results." Her husband attended the first three ceremonies, which included barbecue luncheons, and he joked to the reporters that he was there "to see my frugal wife give away money."

Lyndon did not live to see the extent of his wife's contributions to beautification and conservation. He suffered a series of heart attacks after his retirement from politics. Ten days before his death on January 22, 1973, he and Lady Bird had attended a somber and formal state funeral. On their way back to the ranch, he told her: "When I die, I don't just want our friends who can come in their private planes. I want men in their pick-up trucks and women whose slips hang down below their dresses to be welcome, too."

Lady Bird fulfilled his wishes in death as she did during their almost forty-year marriage. He was buried in the family graveyard next to his parents along the

Pedernales River on the LBJ Ranch, which the Johnsons had given to the people of the United States as a National Historic Site in 1972. Long lines of pick-up trucks and cars filled with neighbors and friends lined up along the road to say goodbye to the man they had supported throughout his political career.

When asked to sum up her years with Lyndon Baines Johnson, the thirty-fifth president, she said: "He made me try harder and do more, and for the natural indolence I had, he was its mortal enemy, and I think perhaps sometimes I made him persevere or take a gentler attitude toward people or events or be less impatient."

For a period of time after Lyndon's death, Lady Bird's health declined. But by the beginning of 1974, she was almost as busy as when she was First Lady. She raised funds for the LBJ Library and Museum in Austin that had been completed and dedicated before LBJ's death. She sponsored symposia on education, the arts, civil rights, women in public life, and environmental issues. She also served on the Board of Regents of the University of Texas. She turned down appointments to the United Nations and did not pursue a political or diplomatic career for which she was qualified. With the exception of campaigning for her son-in-law Charles Robb, she distanced herself from politics. She said, "Politics were Lyndon's life [not mine and] thirty-eight years were enough."

She celebrated her seventieth birthday on December 22, 1982, by giving $125,000 and sixty acres of land on the Colorado River near Austin to establish a National Wildflower Research Center. She called the project her "last hurrah." The research center serves several purposes: to increase interest in the use of native plants; to conduct research into their characteristics and potential; and to serve as a clearing house of information for groups and individuals nationwide. Its goal is "to raise people's awareness of the beauty and value of their local indigenous flowers and shrubs and to help preserve them as a part of our cherished national history."

While research is the priority, the center answers mail from all over the world about wildflowers. The staff compiled fact sheets recommending seed mixes and planting methods for every state and region in the United States. They provide information on seed supplies and resource organizations that can help with local initiatives.

In honor of her contributions to the beautification of America, Secretary of Interior Stewart L. Udall named an island park in the Potomac River the Lady Bird Johnson Park. A second Lady Bird Johnson Park was named in Fredericksburg, Texas, a Hill Country area near the LBJ Ranch that she loves.

When Lady Bird was praised for her work, she said, "I hope through this effort to repay part of the debt I owe for nature's enrichment of my life — my rent, so to speak, for the space I've taken up in the world." She said she wanted her epitaph to read: "SHE PLANTED THREE TREES."

Many historians disagree with Lady Bird's belief that she will be remembered only because of her association with her husband. She taught Americans as she believed that "the loss of beauty diminishes our lives, and its presence enriches us — as individuals and as a nation." Her presence has enriched the lives of an entire nation in her untiring effort to preserve the natural beauty of America.

Afterword

At the publication of this book, Lady Bird lives in Austin and occasionally spends some time on the LBJ Ranch. She says her "greatest pleasure is sharing time with my daughters and seven grandchildren." She also travels, visits art museums, enjoys local scenery, and hikes in the woods, and makes "many more decisions based on my personal pleasure than I did in [Lyndon's] lifetime although I learned to find pleasure in the things that he did. It was learned, not natural."

Lady Bird Johnson
— Courtesy LBJ Library

Time Line

December 22, 1912: Claudia Alta Taylor was born to Thomas J. and Minnie Lee Patillo Taylor in Brick House near Karnack, Texas.

September 14, 1918: Minnie Lee Patillo Taylor died.

May 1928: Graduated from Marshall High School, third in the graduating class.

Fall 1928: Enrolled at St. Mary's Episcopal School for Girls in Dallas, Texas.

Fall 1930: Enrolled at The University of Texas in Austin.

1933: Confirmed at St. David's Episcopal Church.

May 1933: Graduated from The University of Texas with a bachelor of arts degree and a second-grade teacher's certificate.

Fall 1933: Returned to The University of Texas.

May 1934: Received second degree from The University of Texas (journalism).

September 1934: Met Lyndon Baines Johnson.

November 17, 1934: Married Lyndon Baines Johnson in St. Mark's Episcopal Church in San Antonio, Texas.

Fall 1941: Enrolled in business school, Washington, D.C.

Fall 1942: Purchased KTBC, a small radio station in Austin.

March 19, 1944: Birth of first daughter, Lynda Bird Johnson.

July 2, 1947: Birth of second daughter, Lucy Baines Johnson (who later changed the spelling of her name to Luci).

1959: Enrolled in speech class, Washington D.C.

January 1961: Became the Second Lady as wife of Vice-president Lyndon Baines Johnson.

November 22, 1963: Became the First Lady with the assassination of President John F. Kennedy and began diary which was later published.

December 7, 1963: Moved into the White House.

February 11, 1964: First Lady's Committee on the beautification of Washington, D.C. met in the Blue Room of the White House.

February 22, 1965: First interview on the beautification program was published in *U.S. News and World Report.*

March 9, 1965: Planted the first azaleas at the triangle between Maryland and Independence Avenues, at Third Street, S.W.

October 22, 1965: Passage of the Highway Beautification Act.

January 20, 1969: Retired to the LBJ Ranch near Johnson City, Texas.

1970: Published *Lady Bird Johnson: A White House Diary.*

January 22, 1973: Lyndon Baines Johnson died.

December 22, 1982: Gave $125,000 and sixty acres of land to establish a National Wildflower Research Center near Austin, Texas.

Glossary

accredited — certified, approved, endorsed.

aesthetic — enjoyment and appreciation of beauty.

ambassador — a diplomatic (political) agent serving his/her government in a foreign country.

ambition — strong desire for personal advancement.

amphitheater — a level area of circular shape surrounded by rising ground.

anonymity — unknown; of unknown name.

antebellum — existing before the American Civil War.

appalled — horrified, dismayed, shocked.

Appalachia — a region in the eastern United States, in the area of the Appalachian Mountains.

appendicitis — an internal inflammation of a person's appendix; diseased appendix.

appendectomy — surgery to remove a diseased appendix.

assassination — to kill suddenly or secretively; to murder.

bigotry — complete intolerance of persons, beliefs, opinions other than one's own; narrow-minded viewpoint.

bobbed hair — short, straight hairstyle of the 1930s.

Buenos tardes, amigos — Spanish meaning "good afternoon" or "good evening, friends."

campaign — systematic or aggressive activities for a special purpose or to elect a person to an office.

cardiogram — electronic testing of the condition of the heart.

clique — a small, exclusive group of people.

conservation — preservation from loss, decay, injury, or waste.

consort — to associate with.

constituency — the voters or residents in a district represented by an elective officer.

Depression — refers to the Great Depression which began

with the fall of the stock market in 1929 and continued through the 1930s.

deteriorate — to make or become worse; to wear away.

dynasty — a sequence of rulers from the same family; hereditary ruler.

ecology — the branch of biology that deals with the relationship between organisms and their environment.

elocution — a person's manner of speaking or reading in public.

embassy — the official headquarters of an ambassador and his/her staff in a foreign country.

endorse — to approve or support.

enterprises — projects that require boldness and energy; adventure.

entourage — attendants of a person of rank or importance.

epitaph — an inscription on a tomb or mortuary (cemetery) monument.

eradication — completely removed or destroyed.

evaluate — to determine or set the value of; to appraise.

feminist — the doctrine supporting social and political rights of women equal to those of men.

fetid — an offensive odor; stinking.

filibusterer — a person who makes an exceptionally long speech, lasting as long as a day or two, to stop the passing (adoption) of a legislative bill.

foreclose — to deprive a mortgagor the right to redeem his property because of failure to make payments.

gallant — polite, courteous, considerate.

Great Society — the goal of President Lyndon B. Johnson and the Democratic party to establish programs to improve education, provide medical care for the elderly, and eliminate poverty.

gregarious — social, companionable, belonging to a crowd.

impeachment — a formal charge against a public official that, if proven true, removes him/her from office; condemnation.

in-the-black — business term meaning to make a profit.

indefatigable — tireless, untiring, energetic.

indigenous — native, naturalized.

indolence — laziness, slothfulness.

Ku Klux Klan — a secret organization, characterized by white hooded robes, that opposes blacks having equal rights with the white population.

lobbying — a campaign to influence the members of a legislative body to vote for special interest groups.

matrimony — marriage ceremony.

mind set — to think one way without willingness to change.

miscarriage — loss of a child before time for natural birth.

NYA — National Youth Administration, established in 1935, was originally to provide work experience for young men and women between the ages of sixteen and twenty-five who were no longer in school. It later became an agency for student-aid projects which allowed students to work and attend school at the same time.

network affiliation — a transmitting radio or television station, linked by microwave relay, that associates with one major broadcasting company (CBS, ABC, NBC).

nonpartisan — not supporting any of the established parties.

Pearl Harbor — surprise attack by Japan on the U.S. naval base near Honolulu, Hawaii, on December 7, 1941.

peonage — the practice of holding a person in servitude or partial slavery.

pledge — a young woman accepted for membership in a club (sorority), but not yet formally approved.

precinct — a district marked out for governmental purposes; an election district set by boundaries.

psychosomatic — a physical disorder caused by or influenced by the emotional state of the patient.

Reconstruction — the period of time between 1865–1877 when the states that seceded were reorganized as part of the Union after the Civil War.

runoff election — a second vote to determine the winner of a race between the two leading candidates.

ruthless — cruel, merciless.

sanitarium — health resort; private hospital.

segregation — to require the separation of a specific racial, religious, or other group from the general body of society.

sharecropper — a tenant farmer who pays as rent a share (part) of the crop.

sibling rivalry — competition between children of the same parents.

spinster — a woman who has never married.

steely — suggesting strength or hardness.

stock market quotation — statement of the current or market price of a commodity or security.

swindling — cheating a person or business out of money.

symposia — meetings or conferences where several speakers talk on or discuss a topic before an audience.

thrift — economical management; frugal; saving.

tuition — a charge or fee for instruction.

unstinting — no limits or restrictions.

voraciously — eagerly obtains, possesses, or consumes.

wallflower — a person who remains at the side of a party because he/she is shy, unpopular, or has no partner.

WPA — Work Projects Administration (1935–1943), a federal agency that hired persons for public works (roads, bridges, etc.) to relieve national unemployment. Originally Works Progress Administration.

Selected Bibliography

BOOKS:

Boller, Paul F., Jr. *Presidential Wives*. New York: Oxford University Press, 1988.

Caro, Robert A. *The Years of Lyndon Johnson: MEANS OF ASCENT*. New York: Alfred A. Knopf, 1990.

———. *The Years of Lyndon Johnson: THE PATH TO POWER*. New York: Vintage Books, 1983.

Caroli, Betty Boyd. *First Ladies*. New York: Oxford University Press, 1987.

Carpenter, Liz. *Ruffles and Flourishes: the Warm and Tender Story of a Simple Girl Who Found Adventure in the White House*. Garden City, NY: Doubleday & Company, Inc., 1970.

Christian, George. *The President Steps Down: a Personal Memoir of the Transfer of Power*. New York: The Macmillan Company, 1970.

Devaney, John. *Lyndon Baines Johnson, President*. New York: Walker and Company, 1986.

Devine, Robert A., ed. *The Johnson Years, Volume One: Foreign Policy, the Great Society, and the White House*. Lawrence, KS: University Press of Kansas, 1987.

Dugger, Ronnie. *The Politician: The Life and Times of Lyndon Johnson*. New York: W. W. Norton & Company, 1982.

Dunlap, Leslie W. *Our Vice-Presidents and Second Ladies*. Metuchen, NJ: The Scarecrow Press, Inc., 1988.

Gould, Lewis L. *Lady Bird Johnson and the Environment*. Lawrence, KS: The University Press of Kansas, 1988.

Gutin, Myra G. *The President's Partner: The First Lady in the Twentieth Century*. New York: Greenwood Press, 1989.

Hall, Gordon Langley. *Lady Bird and Her Daughters*. Philadelphia: Macrae Smith Company, 1967.

Johnson, Lady Bird. *Texas: A Roadside View*. San Antonio, Texas: Trinity University Press, 1980.

———. *A White House Diary*. New York: Holt, Rinehart and Winston, 1970.

Kellerman, Barbara. *All the President's Kin*. New York: The Free Press, 1981.

Martin, Ralph G. *A Hero for Our Time: an Intimate Story of the Kennedy Years*. New York: Macmillan Publishing Company, 1983.

McConnell, Jane and Burt. *Our First Ladies from Martha Washington to Pat Ryan Nixon*. New York: Thomas Y. Crowell Company, 1969.

Miller, Merle. *Lyndon: an Oral Biography*. New York: Ballantine Books, 1980.

Montgomery, Ruth. *Hail to the Chiefs: My Life and Times with Six Presidents*. New York: Coward-McCann, Inc., 1970.

Smith, Elizabeth Simpson. *Five First Ladies: a Look into the Lives of Nancy Reagan, Rosalynn Carter, Betty Ford, Pat Nixon, and Lady Bird Johnson*. New York: Walker and Company, 1986.

Smith, Marie. *The President's Lady: an Intimate Biography of Mrs. Lyndon B. Johnson*. New York: Random House, 1964.

Steinberg, Alfred. *Sam Johnson's Boy: a Close-Up of the President from Texas*. New York: The Macmillan Company, 1968.

West, J. B. *Upstairs at the White House: My Life with the First Ladies*. New York: Coward, McCann & Geoghegan, Inc., 1973.

White, Theodore H. *The Making of a President, 1964*. New York: Atheneum Publishers, 1965.

Zigler, Edward and Jeanette Valentine, eds. *Project Head Start: A Legacy of the War on Poverty*. New York: Free Press, 1979.

INTERVIEW:

Cox, Ava Johnson. Interview by Jean Flynn, July 6, 1990.

LETTER:

Cindy Wilcox to President Johnson and Family, 7-20-65, "Johnson, Lady Bird" 4/1/65–9/30/65, WHCF Box 62, LBJ Library. Printed with permission of Cindy Wilcox McAnally, Colorado Springs, Colorado.

ORAL HISTORY INTERVIEW TRANSCRIPTS, LBJ Library:

Abell, Bess. Social secretary and assistant to Mrs. Johnson. Three interviews: 37, 24, and 35 pp.

Bolton, Paul. Journalist; long-time employee of KTBC news and personal friend of the Johnsons. Two interviews: 42 and 30 pp.

Carpenter, Elizabeth. Journalist; executive assistant to Vice-president Johnson; press secretary and staff director to Mrs. Johnson. Five interviews: 37, 38, 47, 46, and 33 pp. Retains copyright.

Cooper, Ellen Taylor. Mrs. Johnson's aunt by marriage. Joint interview with Elaine Fischesser. 25 pp.

Fischesser, Elaine. First cousin of Mrs. Johnson. Joint interview with Ellen Taylor Cooper. 25 pp.

Glick, Mrs. Tommy Wurtsbaugh. Sister-in-law of Mrs. Johnson's brother, T. J. Taylor, Jr. 20 pp.

Hirshberg, Henry. San Antonio attorney; best man at LBJ's wedding. 28 pp.

Jones, Luther E., Jr. Student of LBJ's at Sam Houston High School, Houston, Texas; roommate at the Dodge Hotel, Washington, D.C.; Assistant Secretary to U.S. Congressman Richard Kleberg; long-time political associate of LBJ. Two interviews: 28 and 38 pp.

Lasseter, Eugenia Boehringer. Long-time friend of Mrs. Johnson. 35 pp.

McAllister, Gerald N. Canon for the Espicopal Diocese of West Texas; officiated at the wedding of Lynda and Charles Robb. 43 pp.

McElroy, Cameron and Lucille. Friends and East Texas political supporters of the Johnsons; friends of Mrs. Johnson's parents. 18 pp.

Marshall, Cecille Harrison. University of Texas roommate and long-time friend of Mrs. Johnson; maid of honor at the Johnsons' wedding. 22 pp. Retains copyright.

Montgomery, Robert H. Long-time friend of the Johnsons; Professor of Economics, University of Texas at Austin. 32 pp.

Patillo, James Cato, and Nettie Patillo Woodyard. Relatives of Mrs. Johnson. 15 pp.

Powell, Dorris. Long-time Karnack, Texas, friend of Mrs. Johnson. 23 pp.

Quill, Daniel J. Long-time friend and political associate of LBJ; postmaster, San Antonio, Texas. Two interviews: 25

and 34 pp., and one group interview with Oliver Bruck, Sam Fore, Jr., and William S. White, 30 pp.

Rather, Mary. Long-time personal secretary to LBJ and family friend of the Johnsons. Three interviews: 25, 38, and 17 pp. Retains copyright.

Rowe, Elizabeth (Mrs. James H. Rowe). Long-time friend of the Johnsons; chairman, National Capital Planning Commission, 1961–1968. Two interviews: 26 and 21 pp.

Seldon, Emily Crow. College classmate and long-time friend of Mrs. Johnson. Two interviews: 36 and 27 pp.

Taylor, Antonio J. Mrs. Johnson's brother. 35 pp.

Taylor, Willie Day. Long-time LBJ staff member and family friend. 44 pp.

Tooley, Emma Boehringer. High school classmate and personal friend of Mrs. Johnson. 16 pp.

Webb, Terrell Maverick. Widow of Maury Maverick, Sr., and of Walter Prescott Webb; long-time friend of the Johnsons. 42 pp.

Williams, Eugene and Helen. Johnson household employees. 35 pp.

Wright, Zephyr. Johnson family cook, 1942–1969. 47 pp. Retains copyright.

MAGAZINES:

All major periodicals frequently had articles about someone in the Johnson family between the years 1963–1969. Lady Bird granted many interviews during that time to promote her Beautify America campaign. The entries are too numerous to list but are referenced in periodical indexes for that period of time.

Index